T0286916

# BUCKINGHAMSHIRE BUSES

R. J. COOK & K. C. CLOSE

AMBERLEY

First published 2023

Amberley Publishing
The Hill, Stroud,
Gloucestershire, GL5 4EP

www.amberley-books.com

ISBN: 978 1 3981 1437 1 (print)
ISBN: 978 1 3981 1438 8 (ebook)

British Library Cataloguing in Publication Data.
A catalogue record for this book is available from the British Library.

Typeset in 10pt on 13pt Celeste.
Typesetting by SJmagic DESIGN SERVICES, India.
Printed in the UK.

# Contents

# Introduction

Geologically and geographically, Buckinghamshire divides in two parts, as Martin Andrew observed in his book *North Buckinghamshire.* He noted that south of the Chiltern scarp was an inward-looking landscape of beechwoods, sparkling rivers and market towns. Greenline Coaches, passing through, were part of London Transport, terminating in Aylesbury. North Bucks was a place of winding lanes and tiny hamlets, more like the Midlands, of which it is a part. Accordingly, public transport developed to fit and connect the differences. The south was a much prettier place at the start of the twentieth century, expanding beyond suburbia into what became John Betjeman's 'Metro-Land'.

Public transport has struggled to cope with this complexity and change. The south includes sedate towns of Beaconsfield, Maidenhead and Marlow. High Wycombe is home to a major hospital and is south Buckinghamshire's main industrial centre, its population ever swelling. This town, once thriving on its furniture industry, has a busy, bright, town centre bus station and is close to the M40. Milton Keynes outgrew the county, taking over the north to become a unitary authority.

Industry prospered in Aylesbury and the north of county, especially the working-class railway towns of Bletchley and Wolverton. South Buckinghamshire expanded a more affluent population, housing Denham film studios and homes alongside the River Thames. Those people have easy connections to London.

The first wheeled vehicles on British roads appeared in the thirteenth century. People inevitably took lifts in these primitive wagons. Then the stagecoach was invented. Buses derived from stagecoaches but operated over shorter distances. The stagecoach as we know it first appeared on England's roads in the early sixteenth century. It got its name because it travelled in 'stages' of 10 to 15 miles. Stops were usually made at coaching inns where horses would be changed and travellers took a meal and a drink, or stayed overnight.

The first coaches were crude – little more than covered wagons – and were usually drawn by four horses. Without suspension it was a rough ride, at little over 5 mph on rutted tracks on unmade roads. Such travel was impossible in cold or wet weather. Leather strap suspension and other refinements eased the ride, allowing a gradual proliferation of routes. By 1750 there was a basic infrastructure of coaching inns and road improvements funded by turnpikes.

Stagecoach travel was facilitated by improved roads and the turnpike system. Coaches also improved, moving at around 12 mph. Thus, they became expensive and increasingly comfortable. So, with the wealthy on board, Bucks had its share of highwaymen robbing them.

The development of the stagecoach also had a big impact on the postal service. Introduced in 1635, riders carrying the mail rode between 'posts' where the postmaster would take local letters and then hand the remaining letters and any new ones to the next rider. This system was less than perfect: the mail riders were often targeted by robbers and the delivery of the mail was slow.

It was logical to use stagecoaches to carry letters and parcels in a faster, safer and more efficient way. By 1797 there were forty-two coach routes throughout the country, linking most major cities and carrying both stagecoaches and mail coaches.

However, stagecoach long-distance value was usurped by the nineteenth-century railway boom, as were the canals. Buses fared better. 'Bus' is short for 'omnibus', which is reckoned to have been invented by Stanislas Baudry in Nantes. He built a steam-powered flour mill outside the city in 1823. Steam technology produces lots of hot water, and Baudry saw an opportunity to make some money on the side by opening a bathhouse. This was a long

Excursion stop at Winslow's very Dickensian former coaching inn, the old Bell Hotel, in February 2001. Coaching inns had blacksmiths on hand and livery stables.

walk from central Nantes, so to boost custom he had the idea of providing a scheduled shuttle service by coach from the centre of town. It seated eight on a bench on each side. Some passengers used the service for short trips along the route.

Baudry was quick to spot another business opportunity opening up, and launched the first urban transit service in 1826. He expanded the business to Bordeaux the next year, and then to Lyon. His Paris service began in 1829 – the same year as Shillibeer's service in London.

In Britain, it has been argued that John Greenwood was the real inventor of buses, with his service starting in 1824. He was toll-gate keeper in Pendleton on the Manchester to Liverpool turnpike. He bought a horse and cart with several seats, and so began a bus service between those two places.

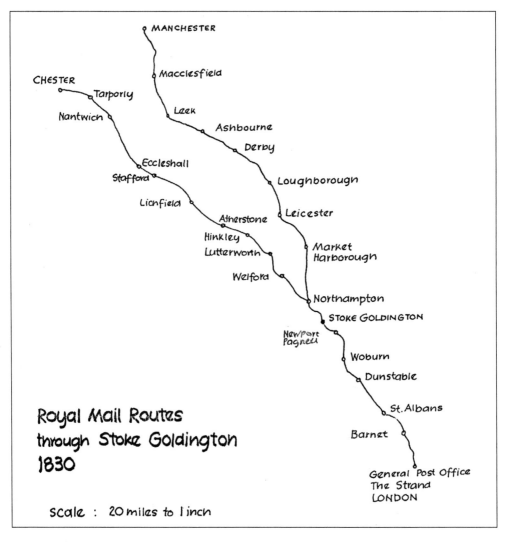

Royal Mail stagecoach routes through North Bucks, 1830. These coaches carried some wealthy people, and Royal Mail was an added attraction for highwaymen. (Map by Andrew Shouler)

Buses and stagecoaches, like early railways, relied on real horse power. Experiments with steam vehicles offered an earlier alternative, but the real breakthrough was when Gottlieb Daimler and Wilhelm Maybach invented the fast-running petrol engine. The London General Omnibus Company ran their first petrol-driven bus in 1899. However, it would be some years before they ousted horses.

London General Omnibus was the dominant provider in the capital, having their own AEC bus-building subsidiary. They consolidated their position during the 1920s in the cut-throat era of pirate operators, such as E. M. Cain, who founded Aylesbury's Red Rover Omnibus Company. They had a comprehensive route network, extending into Buckinghamshire by 1932, and were the precursor to London Transport. By this time one of London's most successful horse bus operators, Thomas Tilling, had taken over a number of successful companies, including Eastern National, which ran services into Aylesbury. These services transferred to another Tilling company, United Counties, in 1952.

No. 6     1932

MAP OF

GENERAL

ROUTES

" To see London there is no point of vantage so good or so cheap as the top of an omnibus, and no city in the world has so many omnibuses."

ISSUED FREE

LONDON GENERAL OMNIBUS C⁰· LᵀᴰMITED.
55, BROADWAY, WESTMINSTER, S.W.1.

WATERLOW & SONS LIMITED, LONDON, DUNSTABLE & WATFORD.

There was a natural progression toward grouping, with two major organisations: British United Traction (BUT) encompassing London Transport, and Thomas Tilling providing the nucleus of a national coordinated bus company, each with their own bus building divisions, AEC and Bristol. By the 1960s this combination was heavily subsidised.

In 1968, the Transport Act was introduced, changing the structure of nationally owned bus companies and creating local government passenger authorities and executives (PTEs).

With the Transport Act of 1985 Britain's bus services were deregulated the following year, then progressively privatised. At its peak in the 1950s the London Transport Executive owned a bus fleet of 8,000 buses – the largest in the world. Now it was to be asset stripped. The Aldenham maintenance works went, along with Routemasters. AEC was by now a cog in the ill-fated Leyland machinery. It was doomed. Remaining larger companies, such as United Counties, which had been bought by Stagecoach, were forcibly split up and sold off between 1986 and 1988.

The National Bus Company National Holidays were first to go, sold to Pleasurama in July 1986. These sales renewed interest in individual liveries and the 'double-N' logo disappeared. National Express was subject to a management buyout, as was the Luton Division of United Counties, which covered Aylesbury depot. Stagecoach was not allowed to own all of United Counties, but bought Midland Red, which operates services from Buckingham to Brackley. Their vehicles are registered in the Midland Red name, but do not use the red livery.

When the company was sold to its management, National Express continued to use the NBC logo until 2003, when it totally disappeared. Most local companies originally went to management buyouts. These were soon bought by emergent large companies, in particular Stagecoach and Arriva.

Amersham's original bus depot, which had been taken over through the creation of London Transport, became a Tesco. Town centre bus depots were worth far more for redevelopment. New depots could replace many on declining industrial estates. More and more people were driving their own cars too, and so there was a shift in demand towards the growing market of school routes.

Stagecoach, which was originally no more than the Souter siblings' sideline, cashed in. Their company took off in Scotland using ex-London expensively refurbished and then discarded Routemasters, which had been sold off cheap by the Tories.

Arriva, then part of the Cowie Group, had grown from the enterprising Tom Cowie's cycle repair business after he was made unemployed as a Sunderland steel worker during the Great Depression. He restored and sold old bikes to desperate job seekers. After the war he got an Italian motor scooter franchise. Using the profits, he bought his first bus. By 1985 his organisation was thriving.

Out of the original five big players, only these two survived as national entities. Stagecoach expanded into the USA, overreaching itself and hitting trouble. Arriva became part of the German DB group. So much for competition. It is a story rather like rail privatisation.

It is against this history and context that the reader should regard the following brief history of Buckinghamshire buses.

# 1

# Early Stages

Apart from going off to war, the average Buckinghamshire person never travelled more than 20 miles from home during the nineteenth century. But there were some long-established Roman routes, notably Ackerman Street (A41) and Watling Street (A5), which meant a regular passage of traders. Another important road cut through the Chiltern Hills, via Wendover.

Many Londoners would soon appreciate the charm of South Bucks as a playground and eventual home, with London Transport offering the means for buses to explore. The Metropolitan Railway led the advance into John Betjeman's 'Metro-Land'. The company foresaw suburbia, buying up land along their railway line. Charabanc excursions also paved the way for a proliferation of bus routes and expanding settlements beyond suburbia. On the plus side, this ease of travel would ultimately encourage progress in transport and communication.

Buckinghamshire is blessed by the passage of the mature meanderings of the River Thames, adding beauty to the attractive old town of Marlow – along with a name for the county's police force. As such, boats were another valued mode of travel down to London or west towards Gloucestershire.

Of course, in these modern times few of the wealthy use buses. But in those early stages of public transport, travel by stagecoach was expensive and very much for the privileged.

The first stagecoach route began in 1610 and ran from Edinburgh to Leith. Early stagecoaches were slow, taking eight days in 1673 to travel from London to Exeter. Formation of a stage company in 1706 established a regular coach route between York and London. Regular coach service routes thus proliferated.

In 1754, a company in Manchester began a new service called the 'Flying Coach', which it claimed would (barring accidents!) travel from Manchester to London in just four and a half days. A similar service began from Liverpool three years later, using coaches with the new steel spring suspension. These coaches reached the great speed of 8 mph and completed the journey to London in just three days.

A stage ran west through Beaconsfield, then a small town of 1,110 people. It became home to Edmund Burke, a Dublin-born statesman, which when connected by railway expanded into a place of affluence. These days the main road through Beaconsfield sees an

The first stagecoaches were little more than covered wagons, generally drawn by four horses. Without suspension, they could only travel at around 5 mph on the rutted tracks and unmade roads of the time. This grand, hand-crafted stagecoach pulled by a magnificent team of four had visited the 2000 Boxing Day meet of Bicester & Whaddon Chase Hunt in Winslow's Home Close. It is an image of overwhelming horse power that looks as if it is bursting out from the page. The coach and horses belong to the Devil's Horsemen, who provide horses and skilled riders for films and TV and are based in nearby Mursley.

almost constant stream of traffic. There are posh shops, including boutiques, where if you have to ask the price of anything you can't afford it.

By the late 1600s the area was prowled by highwaymen, who robbed stagecoaches going in both directions. The Royal Saracen's Hotel is a stately reminder of those dangerous days, where coaches would change horses and passengers could rest overnight. The rambling old building is a memorial to a bygone but notable age in the history of bus travel.

The last Buckinghamshire stagecoach in Bucks ran from Wendover, in the Chiltern foothills, to London in 1890, by which time railways were established, pioneered by enlightened local magnates. Before the railway came to Amersham and Chesham, the London & North Western Railway (LNWR) coach plied between Berkhamsted via Chesham and the Hockeridges. It departed from the George & Dragon in High Street, Chesham.

The year 1910 saw a breakthrough for British bus design. This was the famous London General AEC B type – petrol engined, open-top deck and very reliable. It carried thirty-four passengers. They were so robust that the War Office sent 900 of them to France for service as troop carriers during the First World War. One, numbered B43, was affectionately known as *Ole Bill*; it cruised at 16 mph.

AEC were working steadily to improve bus design, with provincial vehicle builders joining the race. Advance was rapid, with the new oil engines delivering more power if less speed. Few people realise that the true inventor of the oil engine was a Scotsman working in a Fenny Stratford backstreet workshop.

Vehicle design made a quantum leap forward between 1925 and 1930. Pneumatic tyres, lightweight chassis, improved brakes and transmissions, arterial roads and better surfaces were revolutionary. The Bucks County Structure plan of 1935 established plans for bypasses.

*Above*: Two very full National charabancs on Winslow's Bell Corner await departure to Windsor on a Women's Institute outing. Windsor used to be right on the county border and is still a popular tourist attraction.

*Right*: GWR proposals to build a Windsor connection were accepted in 1847, on a promise that the company would fund improvements to roads and bridges. This small Marlow & District Motor Company worked in association with them.

MARLOW & DISTRICT MOTOR SERVICES, Ltd.

Official Time Table

(in association with the Great Western Railway Company)

commencing
JUNE 4th, 1932

## MAIDENHEAD STATION, MARLOW ROAD CORNER, CRAUFURD ARCH, BELMONT STORES, BELMONT CRESCENT, SEELEY'S STORES

|  | | | | | | | | | | | | | | | | |
|---|---|---|---|---|---|---|---|---|---|---|---|---|---|---|---|---|
| Seeley's Stores... | 7*39 | 8*9 | 8*46 | 9*10 | 9*32 | 10*10 | 1035 | 11 0 | 1122 | 12 0 | 1230 | 1250 | 1*30 | 150 | 230 |
| Belm'nt Crescent | 7 41 | 811 | 8 48 | 9 12 | 9 34 | 10 12 | 1037 | 11 2 | 1124 | 12 2 | 1232 | 1252 | 1 32 | 152 | 232 |
| Belm'nt Stores... | 7 42 | 812 | 8 49 | 9 13 | 9 35 | 10 13 | 1038 | 11 3 | 1125 | 12 3 | 1233 | 1253 | 1 33 | 153 | 233 |
| Craufurd Arch... | 7 44 | 814 | 8 51 | 9 15 | 9 37 | 10 15 | 1040 | 11 5 | 1127 | 12 5 | 1235 | 1255 | 1 35 | 155 | 235 |
| Marlow Rd. Cor. | 7 46 | 816 | 8 53 | 9 17 | 9 39 | 10 17 | 1042 | 11 7 | 1129 | 12 7 | 1237 | 1257 | 1 37 | 157 | 237 |
| Maidenhead Sta. | 7 47 | 817 | 8 54 | 9 18 | 9 40 | 10 18 | 1043 | 11 8 | 1130 | 12 8 | 1238 | 1258 | 1 38 | 158 | 238 |

|  | | | | | | | | | | | | | | | | | | |
|---|---|---|---|---|---|---|---|---|---|---|---|---|---|---|---|---|---|---|
| Seeley's Stores... | 3 0 | 3 30 | 4 0 | 430 | 450 | 515 | 545 | 610 | 635 | 7 0 | 720 | 745 | 810 | 840 | 915 | 938 | 10 0 | 1020 |
| Belm'nt Crescent | 3 2 | 3 32 | 4 2 | 432 | 452 | 517 | 547 | 612 | 637 | 7 2 | 722 | 747 | 812 | 842 | 917 | 940 | 10 2 | 1022 |
| Belm'nt Stores... | 3 3 | 3 33 | 4 3 | 433 | 453 | 518 | 548 | 613 | 638 | 7 3 | 723 | 748 | 813 | 843 | 918 | 941 | 10 3 | 1023 |
| Craufurd Arch... | 3 5 | 3 35 | 4 5 | 435 | 455 | 520 | 550 | 615 | 640 | 7 5 | 725 | 750 | 815 | 845 | 920 | 943 | 10 5 | 1025 |
| Marlow Rd. Cor. | 3 7 | 3 37 | 4 7 | 437 | 457 | 522 | 552 | 617 | 642 | 7 7 | 727 | 752 | 817 | 847 | 922 | 945 | 10 7 | 1027 |
| Maidenhead Sta. | 3 8 | 3 38 | 4 8 | 438 | 458 | 523 | 553 | 618 | 643 | 7 8 | 728 | 753 | 818 | 848 | 923 | 946 | 10 8 | 1028 |

|  | | | | | | | | | | | | | | | |
|---|---|---|---|---|---|---|---|---|---|---|---|---|---|---|---|
| Maidenhead Sta. | 7*55 | 8*25 | 9*0 | 9*20 | 9*45 | 10*20 | 1045 | 1110 | 1145 | 1215 | 1240 | 1 5 | 1*40 | 215 | 245 |
| Marlow Rd. Cor. | 7 56 | 8 26 | 9 1 | 9 21 | 9 46 | 10 21 | 1046 | 1111 | 1146 | 1216 | 1241 | 1 6 | 1 41 | 216 | 246 |
| Craufurd Arch... | 7 58 | 8 28 | 9 3 | 9 23 | 9 48 | 10 23 | 1048 | 1113 | 1148 | 1218 | 1243 | 1 8 | 1 43 | 218 | 248 |
| Belm'nt Stores... | 8 0 | 8 30 | 9 5 | 9 25 | 9 50 | 10 25 | 1050 | 1115 | 1150 | 1220 | 1245 | 1 10 | 1 45 | 220 | 250 |
| Belm'nt Crescent | 8 1 | 8 31 | 9 6 | 9 26 | 9 51 | 10 26 | 1051 | 1116 | 1151 | 1221 | 1246 | 1 11 | 1 46 | 221 | 251 |
| Seeley's Stores... | 8 3 | 8 33 | 9 8 | 9 28 | 9 53 | 10 28 | 1053 | 1118 | 1153 | 1223 | 1248 | 1 13 | 1 48 | 223 | 253 |

|  | | | | | | | | | | | | | | | | | | |
|---|---|---|---|---|---|---|---|---|---|---|---|---|---|---|---|---|---|---|
| Maidenhead Sta. | 315 | 345 | 410 | 440 | 5 5 | 530 | 6 0 | 625 | 645 | 710 | 730 | 755 | 825 | 9 0 | 925 | 950 | 1010 | 10 30 |
| Marlow Rd. Cor. | 316 | 346 | 411 | 441 | 5 6 | 531 | 6 1 | 626 | 646 | 711 | 731 | 756 | 826 | 9 1 | 926 | 951 | 1011 | 10 31 |
| Craufurd Arch... | 318 | 348 | 413 | 443 | 5 8 | 533 | 6 3 | 628 | 648 | 713 | 733 | 758 | 828 | 9 3 | 928 | 953 | 1013 | 10 33 |
| Belm'nt Stores... | 320 | 350 | 415 | 445 | 510 | 535 | 6 5 | 630 | 650 | 715 | 735 | 8 0 | 830 | 9 5 | 930 | 955 | 1015 | 10 35 |
| Belm'nt Crescent | 321 | 351 | 416 | 446 | 511 | 536 | 6 6 | 631 | 651 | 716 | 736 | 8 1 | 831 | 9 6 | 931 | 956 | 1016 | 10 36 |
| Seeley's Stores... | 323 | 353 | 418 | 448 | 513 | 538 | 6 8 | 633 | 653 | 718 | 738 | 8 3 | 833 | 9 8 | 933 | 958 | 1018 | 10†38 |

\* Not Sundays  † and then to Marlow

An extract from Marlow & District's 1932 timetable.

# 2
# Capital Ideas

Buckinghamshire's bus history is intimately linked with the capital, past and present, political and practical. London is different with current subsidies, but direct mention and comparison with the outcome of 1985 deregulation is essential to correct understanding – a point returned to in Chapter 8. Ripples and tides from London have massive effects on immediate neighbours.

L.G. OMNIBUS ARRIVING AT "WINGROVES" TEA GARDENS, BURNHAM BEECHES.

Burnham Beeches, near Slough and Maidenhead, is a very affluent part of the county with excellent hotels and golf courses. Slough was removed from the county and derided by Betjeman's wonderful line: 'Come friendly bombs and fall on Slough, it isn't fit for humans now.' When this picture was taken the area was a haven for escape, with simple pleasures away from congested, polluted post-First World War London. It was soon colonised by people who didn't want city or suburb.

Those of us growing up in the twentieth century could not imagine a life without buses. Their rapid development in the capital, with London General Omnibus and Tilling spreading routes outwards into Buckinghamshire, supported massive population growth, which was also accelerated by railways. The B-type bus changed the way of travel across the county and its technology was mimicked by others, notably Leyland.

South Bucks in particular developed rapidly in the early twentieth century due to its proximity to London. Over the years this region has experienced affluent overspill, including actors and film stars in country mansions. Denham was renowned for its film studios, with an elite aerodrome ferrying the stars in and out. It is perhaps therefore not surprising that it does not abound with bus services. Capital ideas made South Bucks what it is today, but the world is changing, and this county of the larger motor car will be changing with it.

IN & AROUND
LONDON
BY
LONDON'S UNDERGROUND
SUMMER 1932

*Left*: Of course, London remained a style beacon for the better off, so Buckinghamshire newcomers used advancing transport systems to enjoy the best of both worlds.

*Opposite*: This Leyland Express coach was a direct descendant of the stagecoaches. There was money to be made and men like E. M. Cain were eager to chance their arm. Aylesbury, Buckinghamshire's county town, attracted many to start express services. Cain was one such, choosing Aylesbury as his express coach destination because he had an aunt living there – she ran the booking office. London General's Greenline Coaches would usurp them all by nationalisation following the 1933 Transport Act. Green Line's origin was in a network of limited-stop coach services started by the London General Omnibus Company in the late 1920s that operated between London and towns within about a 30-mile radius. That radius extended after 1933, reaching Aylesbury.

# LONDON–AYLESBURY
# LONDON–CHESHAM
## SERVICES

TRAVEL BY COACH—BUT

# BE SURE IT'S
# WEST LONDON

*See inside for details.*

# List of Agents.

**LONDON**

London Coastal Coaches Ltd, 'Victoria Coach Station,' Buckingham Palace Road, S.W.1 ('Phone: VICTORIA 2766 [70 lines]).
7b Lower Belgrave Street, Victoria, S.W.1.
433 Brixton Road, S.W.9.
7 South Side, Clapham, S.W. 4.
All Keith Prowse, District Messenger and Pickfords offices.
Chas. Rickards Ltd, 12 Spring Street, W.2.
Morffew's Travel Bureau, 19 Edgware Road, W.2
Regal Travel Bureau, 121 Edgware Road, W.2.
and all 'London Coastal' Agents.

### Look for the 'London Coastal' Sign.

**LONDON PICKING-UP POINTS**

Victoria Coach Station, Buckingham Palace Road, S.W.1.
Marble Arch, The Mitre, Seymour Street
Craven Park, St. Michael & All Angels' Church.
Harrow, College Road (between Clarendon Road and Headstone Road).

NOTE—*In the Metropolitan Traffic Area* passengers will not be picked up at any point other than those shown above

Passengers may alight at any point

RICKMANSWORTH: Post Office (*Agent*: Mrs. Neale, 5 Station Road. 'Phone: 622)
AMERSHAM (NEW TOWN): Sycamore Library (*Agent*: Mr. Woods, Sycamore Library. 'Phone: 250)
AMERSHAM (OLD TOWN): The Red House Tea Shop, Market Square.
CHESHAM: Broadway (*Agent*: H. G. Goss, High Street. 'Phone: 241)
GREAT MISSENDEN: White Lion (*Agent*: Mr. Davey, White Lion. 'Phone: 114)
WENDOVER: Post Office (*Agent*: T. Carter & Sons, High Street 'Phone: )

Garages, Buckingham Street. 'Phone: 123)
Sub-Agents: The Aylesbury Motor Co. Ltd, Kingsbury Square (Phone: 87)
S. G. Water, High Street and Market Square ('Phone: 238)
A. T. Adkins, 120 High Street ('Phone: 215)

**CONDITIONS**

INTERMEDIATE TICKETS.—Seats are not guaranteed on intermediate journeys
RETURN TICKETS.—Return journeys must be booked in advance.
LUGGAGE.—Hand baggage only, at passengers' risk.
DOGS.—1/- any single journey. Carried only at driver's discretion and owner's risk.
CHILDREN.—Infants under 3, carried free. Between 3 and 14, half fare; fractions of 6d. charged as 6d. (1/- minimum fare)
*No seat guaranteed unless full fare paid*
TICKETS.—Mutilated, torn or defaced tickets will not be accepted.
The Company shall not be held responsible for losses or additional expenses due to delays, changes in service, sickness, weather, strikes, or other causes. Although every effort will be made to secure punctuality, same cannot be guaranteed. Refunds will only be made in special cases, and the liability shall not extend beyond the value of the unused portion of the ticket returned

*For further information, write or 'phone*

# WEST - LONDON - COACHES

### 202 SUTHERLAND AVENUE
### MAIDA VALE, LONDON, W.9
### ABERCORN 1074

June 1st, 1932.

Express coach tickets were sold by agencies. Here we see a list of those serving West London Coaches.

*Above*: Local bus services were operated by rather uncomfortable-looking vehicles until the advances of the late 1920s. The Model T was a capital idea, robust and versatile. It would have seemed very modern at the time.

*Right*: Amersham-on-the-Hill is distinct from the town of Amersham, but the whole area has a reputation for affluence, with much spilling in from London in the 1920s. Rural living gave way to the more sophisticated. The Metropolitan Railway bought a lot of local land with a view to extending customer base. Rising populations encouraged bus operators, Amersham & District being the most successful. This image is an advertisement for the company services and modern AEC Regal coaches.

Official **TIME TABLE**

*Registered Offices* BROADWAY AMERSHAM Phone : 36

**AMERSHAM**
—— AND DISTRICT ——
**MOTOR BUS &**
**HAULAGE C̣o. L̲ᵀᴰ**

OCT. 20th to NOV. 30th, 1932     One Penny

# H. GODDARD & SONS

*Furnishers and Outfitters*

A visit to our new and spacious
Showrooms is cordially invited

*Removals and Storage*

## 65 William St., SLOUGH

'PHONE 247

Printed by Index Publishers (Dunstable) Ltd., for Amersham and District Motor Bus and Haulage Co., Ltd., Amersham, Bucks.

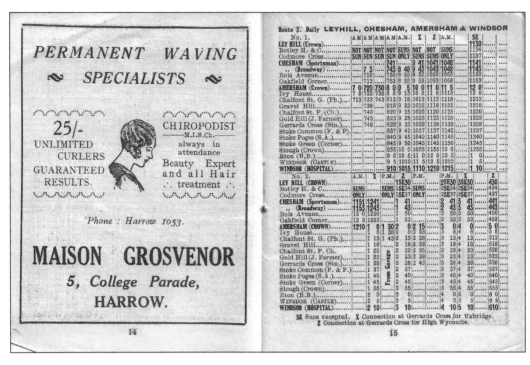

Extract from Amersham & District's timetable with atmospheric period advertising.

Amersham & District Strachan-bodied AEC Regal parked by its Windsor Castle destination in the early 1930s. The company would soon be engulfed by LGOC's Greenline Operations. The state-backed concept was to standardise London's express coach services.

# 3

# County Rules

This chapter explains how Aylesbury became the focus of cross-county travel despite being far north in the county, as it was perfectly situated on the Roman Akeman Street (A41).

Buckingham gave its name to one of King Alfred's new counties that were organised to defend his kingdom. The district went on to prosper with the growing wool trade. Buckinghamshire took its name from Buckingham, meaning 'Bucca's town'. Buckinghamshire meant 'Bucca's share'.

When the Normans came they imposed a new social order called feudalism. Whatever the cruelties, the new regime was at least relieved by better architecture. England's historic counties were re-established for administration by the Normans. They existed, headed by sheriffs, to enforce laws. These became lord lieutenants. Some counties were based on earlier Anglo-Saxon kingdoms and shires. They served administrative functions, defining local culture. This situation was formalised in 1889 with the red-brick County Office building in Walton Street built in 1921. It was a powerful symbol of a reforming municipal age.

Long before counties became administrative centres in 1889, however, Henry VIII moved Buckinghamshire's administrative centre south to Aylesbury. This was to honour his new father-in-law, lord of Aylesbury Manor, George Boleyn.

Aylesbury, situated in on the rich soils of the Vale, just north of the picturesque Chilterns, was a thriving marketplace for local farms and much more. It was the natural focus for transport, made more convenient by location on the aforementioned road south to London and the one west to Gloucestershire and Bath. Originally, people either walked or rode carrier's carts into town. Buses were the next inevitable step.

Prior to the creation of the DVLA in the 1970s, and then VOSA, public service vehicle operators, vehicle registrations and driving licences were administered by local authorities. As population and traffic expanded in the 1960s and 1970s along with vehicle technology and size changes, rules were devolved by government to the specialist administrative centres in South Wales. Commercial vehicles became subject to the tachograph, but buses were exempt. As far as transport was concerned, matters were now a matter of state rules, although taxi licences were still the provenance of county councils.

The Aylesbury that R. J. Cook recalls from childhood is a world away from today. In the 1950s and 1960s buses thronged the town centre, before bus traffic was driven underground to the bus station beneath the Friars Shopping Centre. Much of the old town centre was destroyed to make way for this.

The new bus station opened in 1968, but there was still the problem of buses driving through the busy Market Square. There was even a terrible accident when a woman shopping for her daughter was run over and killed by a bus driving through the area. Nicholas Brooks reported in the *Bucks Herald* on 2 January 2002:

Shoppers will still be dodging buses in Aylesbury Market Square for years to come, even though the campaign to kick them out is already more than a decade old. Calls to shift buses out of the heart of the town started with it being semi pedestrianised in the late 1980s, but last week's joint meeting between district and county councillors kicked the issue into the long grass again. 'More research' was needed, the meeting was told. Officers for both authorities reported that the question of public transport was now tangled up with the future redevelopment of large stretches of central Aylesbury, and cannot be tackled until councillors have an idea of what the town will eventually look like – yet more months or even years ahead.

Bedgrove's Councillor Chester Jones said, 'For crying out loud, it's all about what the bus companies think.' Meanwhile, controversial rising bollards continued to keep cars out of the Market Square.

Aylesbury Market Square, *c.* 1920. Carrier's carts brought people to town on market days. It was not the official bus station, though one vehicle has found room to park here in this quaint picture of rural majesty.

Kingsbury Square, *c.* 1920. Buses were ramshackle affairs when organisation was in its infancy. C. H. Cherry was a local pioneer based in Waddesdon. His business was taken over by Keith Coaches/Red Rover in 1933.

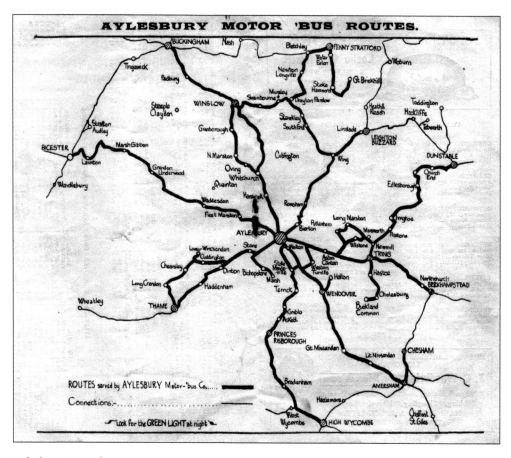

Aylesbury Motor bus route map.

A Queen's Park Coaches utility bodies a Dennis shortly before a paint job officially made it a member of the Tilling Eastern National fleet, *c.* 1952. It is heading off to RAF Halton Camp near Wendover. National service meant that the town's buses were kept busy with servicemen, as they had been a few years earlier during the Second World War.

Eastern National wasted little time with oddball vehicles like the Dennis, renewing its fleet with the latest from Tilling's in-house bus builder Bristol, with the usual ECW coachwork from Lowestoft. (Colin Seabright)

One of the City of Oxford Motor Services (COMS) bright, modern AEC Regent Vs before departing on the pleasant Oxford service 82, via Thame, in 1963. They were rather bouncy according to R. J. Cook's recollection. (R. H. G. Simpson)

A colourful, mid-1950s view of the through road passing Kingsbury Square and two AEC Regent buses. COMS were in the BUT grouping that favoured AEC and was renowned for an attractive livery and clean buses, as befitting their varsity home city. Their 82 Oxford service is passing one of Red Rover's ex-London Transport RTs. (Colin Seabright)

The Dennis Lance K3 was the last new bus purchased by E. M. Cain in 1951. It is seen here ready for the company's long run to Buckingham, a route then shared with Eastern National of the Tilling Group. (R. H. G. Simpson)

Aylesbury bus station, c. 1998, before the revamp. Arriva's Buckingham service 66 stands in the foreground, carrying their local 'Aylesbury & the Vale' livery.

This well-cared-for COMS AEC Regal shows the diversity of routes plying out of and arriving in mid-1950s Aylesbury. Red Rover's inspector consults with a driver, and we catch a glimpse of a Thames Valley Bristol Lodekka in the sunny background. (R. H. G. Simpson)

Passing across the top of Market Square is number 104 in the United Counties (UCOC) fleet list, a 1956 Bristol LS5G. It is Amersham-bound, 20 miles away, and heading off Kingsbury Square. There was no ring road at this time. Aylesbury was UCOC's most southerly depot and Amersham was on the edge of London's Metroland – also reached by Tilling's Thames Valley and London Transport.

Stuart Mills bought Red Rover in 1955. The company's optimism about the future of public transport in the 1960s accounted for them purchasing three seventy-one-seater AEC buses in the 1960s. This picture shows their second AEC Bridgemaster on Saturday 4 September 1971 as it approaches the Belgrave Road terminus, near Carlton Close. New housing growth was and still is prolific in the county town. The same scene today would see few buses and lots of parked cars.

Kingsbury Square on a summer Saturday afternoon in the early 1960s – judging by the crowds. The 301 London Transport (yet to be repackaged London Country) and poppy red Thames Valley Bristol K5G High Wycombe service are lined up behind the Red Rover.

New to the company in 1962, Red Rover's first AEC Bridgemaster, with air suspension, glides through Kingsbury Square in the 1960s. (Colin Seabright)

Red Rover YMT on a shopping service to the new Raban's Lane Tesco in the early 1980s. (Tom Goodwin)

*Above*: Ex-London Transport DMS on the Stoke Mandeville Hospital run, winter 1985. (Tom Goodwin)

*Below*: A two-door Leyland National passes the controversial Blue Leanie Insurance building near the exit to Wendover Road in June 1985. (P. Bungay)

*Above*: Red Rover Keith Coach on service, Kingsbury Square 1985. (P. Bungay)

*Below*: A Red Rover Leyland Leopard heading out from the Friars bus station to a non-designated destination, *c.* 1985. (P. Bungay)

*Above*: Two Leyland Nationals parked at Red Rover's Bicester Road depot in the 1980s. These vehicles were meant to be the latest answer to urban transport, but London Transport and other corporations could not get rid of them fast enough. Passengers complained of excessive noise. British Leyland were on a downward spiral of failure and fire sale privatisation. (Tom Goodwin)

*Below*: A sunny day in Aylesbury's Kingsbury in 1985. Red Rover liked their DMS types, but they were not well suited to London Transport, who sold them off rather cheaply. Off-the-peg buses never quite worked for London, but the DMS handled rural ways well. (P. Bungay)

End of an era. Ex-UCOC Bristol VR pretending to be a Red Rover in the Stoke Mandeville parking bay, summer 1988. (Tom Goodwin)

# 4

# Greenways

Famed bus designer J. G. Rackham left Leyland in the 1930s to work for the Yellow Coach Company in the United States and experienced General Motors' advances, including semi-automatic transmission and rear engines. He created a new range of buses on his return, working for AEC, which established close links with Leyland in building London's buses. The AEC Regal and Leyland Titan set new standards. London General Omnibus formed a subsidiary called Greenline. Up until then local authorities like Bucks had issued operators' licences. There had been no coordination. Greenline standardised services with identical T-type (Titan) coaches. Rival operators had to follow suit, but their days were numbered on Home Counties routes because Greenline did not like competition.

Though the still rural Home Counties were shielded from the worst of interwar depression, the brief Labour government interlude favoured state ownership. The first wave of nationalisation was with the London Transport Act of 1933. It absorbed Greenline and London's green buses, which appeared as far north as Aylesbury, taking over the Amersham & District depot in Amersham.

This Act was also used to take over Red Rover's express London route. So, E. M. Cain, having bought Young's Aylesbury Motor Bus Company, then focused his small private company on a route jointly operated with Tilling. After the Second World War, Red Rover developed new local town routes. Aylesbury became a post-war designated London overspill 'expanded town'.

Challenges of operating rural bus services were simple in an age of high demand with low car ownership. New car sales were restricted to boost exports. However, all the pent-up demand and hire purchase facilities created the late 1950s boom when Prime Minister Harold Macmillan told voters, 'You've never had it so good.'

Greenline Coaches of the 706 and 707 routes were a familiar sight parked in Buckingham Street. Sadly, they are no more. New services nowadays abound. The Aylesbury–London Greenline 706 service started in November 1932. Two vintage vehicles – an RMC double-decker of a type never used on the route and a preserved AEC Regal IV RF type – ran seventieth anniversary services for a celebration in 2002. The sturdy RF types had remained in service until 1972.

*Above*: London Transport Greenline AEC Regal IV RF parked in Buckingham Street outside Agro Electrical premises, *c.* 1954. Greenline services took over E. M. Cain's Red Rover in the early 1930s following nationalisation of express services into and around the capital. The RF entered service in 1972. (R. H. G. Simpson)

*Below*: Winterhill, Milton Keynes, then the National Bus Company depot, seen here on an open day on Saturday 19 May 1985. Two of London's green buses, of the type running into Aylesbury until the late 1960s, are in the centre – a Regal IV coach and RT double-decker. (Andrew Shouler)

*Above*: Chiltern Bus Company's immaculate Leyland TD1, 1932.

*Left*: Chiltern Bus' May 1935 timetable. Buses were increasingly important around the ever-expanding High Wycombe and Maidenhead.

## HIGH WYCOMBE — SANDS — LANE END

| | NSS | NS | NSS | NS | NS | WO | SU | NS | NS | SU | SO | NS | | |
|---|---|---|---|---|---|---|---|---|---|---|---|---|---|---|
| H. WYCOMBE (Qn. Vic. Rd.) | 7 6 | 7 30 | 8 0 | 8 30 | 9 5 | 9 25 | 10 30 | 10 55 | 12 0 | 12 0 | 12 25 | 1 0 | 1 55 | 2 25 |
| DOWNLEY TURN | 7 13 | 7 37 | 8 7 | 8 37 | 9 12 | 9 32 | 10 37 | 11 2 | ... | 12 7 | 12 32 | 1 7 | 2 1 | 1 32 |
| EATON AVENUE | | | | | | | | | 12 6 | | | | | |
| SANDS, HOUR GLASS | 7 15 | 7 39 | 8 9 | 8 39 | 9 14 | 9 34 | 10 39 | 11 4 | 12 8 | 12 9 | 12 34 | 1 9 | 2 4 | 2 34 |
| BOOKER CORNER | 7 19 | 7 43 | 8 13 | 8 43 | 9 18 | 9 38 | 10 43 | 11 8 | 12 12 | 12 13 | 12 38 | 1 13 | 2 8 | 2 39 |
| RED BARN | | | | | | | | | | | | | | |
| PARK LANE | 7 24 | 7 48 | 8 18 | 8 48 | 9 23 | 9 43 | 10 48 | 11 13 | 12 17 | 12 18 | 12 43 | 1 18 | 2 13 | 2 43 |
| LANE END (Old Sun) | 7 29 | 7 53 | 8 23 | 8 53 | 9 28 | 9 48 | 10 53 | 11 18 | 12 22 | 12 23 | 12 48 | 1 23 | 2 18 | 2 48 |
| LANE END (Moor Farm) | | | | | | | | | | | | | | |

| | FSS | SO | NSS | FSS | NS | | | SSO | NSS | | NS | SU | |
|---|---|---|---|---|---|---|---|---|---|---|---|---|---|
| H. WYCOMBE (Qn. Vic. Rd.) | 2 55 | 3 25 | 3 55 | 4 2 | 4 25 | 4 55 | 5 25 | 5 55 | 6 2 | | 6 30 | 6 30 | |
| DOWNLEY TURN | 3 2 | 3 32 | 4 2 | 4 9 | 4 32 | 5 2 | 5 32 | 6 2 | 6 9 | | | 6 37 | |
| EATON AVENUE | | | | | | | | | | | 6 36 | | |
| SANDS, HOUR GLASS | 3 4 | 3 34 | 4 4 | 4 11 | 4 34 | 5 4 | 5 34 | 6 4 | 6 11 | | 5 38 | 6 39 | |
| BOOKER CORNER | 3 8 | 3 38 | 4 8 | 4 15 | 4 38 | 5 8 | 5W38 | 6 8 | 6 15 | | 6 42 | 6 43 | |
| RED BARN | | | | | | | | | | | | | |
| PARK LANE | 3 13 | 3 43 | 4 13 | 4 20 | 4 43 | 5 13 | 5 43 | 6 13 | 6 20 | | 6 47 | 6 48 | |
| LANE END (Old Sun) | 3 18 | 3 48 | 4 18 | 4 25 | 4 48 | 5 18 | 5 48 | 6 18 | 6 25 | | 6 53 | 6 53 | |
| LANE END (Moor Farm) | | | | | | | | | | | 6 55 | | |

| | | | NS | SU | | | SSO | | | SSO | | |
|---|---|---|---|---|---|---|---|---|---|---|---|---|
| H. WYCOMBE (Qn. Vic. Rd.) | 7 0 | ... | 7 30 | 7 55 | 7§55 | | 8 25 | 8§55 | 9 25 | | 9 55 | 10 30 |
| DOWNLEY TURN | 7 7 | ... | 7 37 | 8 2 | 8§2 | | 8 32 | 9§2 | 9 32 | | 10 2 | 10 37 |
| EATON AVENUE | | | | | | | | | | | | |
| SANDS, HOUR GLASS | 7 9 | ... | 7 39 | 8 4 | 8§4 | | 8 34 | 9§4 | 9 34 | | 10 4 | 10 39 |
| BOOKER CORNER | 7 13 | ... | 7 43 | 8 9 | 8§8 | | 8 39 | 9§8 | 9 38 | | 10 8 | 10 43 |
| RED BARN | | | | 8 14 | | | | | | | | |
| PARK LANE | 7 18 | ... | 7 48 | | 8§13 | | 8 43 | 9§13 | 9 43 | | 10 13 | 10 48 |
| LANE END (Old Sun) | 7 23 | ... | 7 53 | 8 19 | 8§18 | | 8 48 | 9§18 | 9 48 | | 10 18 | 10 53 |
| LANE END (Moor Farm) | | | | | | | | | | | | 10‡55 |

**FSO**—Friday and Saturday only.    **FSS**—Friday, Saturday and Sunday only.    **NS or ‡**—Not Sunday.
**NSS**—Not Saturday and Sunday.    **SSO**—Saturday and Sunday only.    **SU**—Sunday only.
**WO**—Wednesday only.    **SO**—Saturday only.    **W**—Wednesday and Sunday only.
**§**—Operates on Sundays from 1st Sunday in May to 2nd Sunday in September only, inclusive.

*Above*: An extract from the Chiltern Bus Company timetable, 1935.

*Below*: Bus fare stages, 1935 – there were 240d in £1.

## From GREEN LINE COACH STATION
Poland Street, near Oxford Circus.   Gerrard 2101
### and OXFORD CIRCUS

| Route Letter | TO | Service Interval and Through Fares |
|---|---|---|
| C | *CHERTSEY, Via Piccadilly, Hammersmith, Richmond, Kingston, Dittons, Hurst Park, Molesey, Walton, Weybridge, (for Brooklands) Addlestone | 30 mins. 2/3 Single 3/6 Return |
| D | DORKING. Via Gt. Scotland Yard, Kennington, Stockwell, Clapham, Balham, Tooting, Morden, Ewell, Epsom, Ashtead, Leatherhead, Mickleham, Boxhill | 30 mins. 2/- Single 3/- Return |
| F | †HERTFORD. Via Camden Town, Finsbury Park, Wood Green, Enfield, Ponders End, Waltham Cross, Cheshunt, Wormley, Broxbourne, Hoddesdon, Ware | 30 mins. 1/6 Single 2/6 Return |
| G | *GUILDFORD. Via Shepherds Bush, Hammersmith, Barnes, Roehampton, Kingston-by-pass, Sandown Park, Esher, Cobham, Wisley, Ripley, Burpham | 30 mins. 2/- Single 3/6 Return |
| I | FARNINGHAM. Via Great Scotland Yard, Elephant & Castle, New Cross, Lewisham, Lee Green, Eltham, Sidcup, Foots Cray, Birchwood, Swanley Junction | 60 mins. 1/9 Single 2/9 Return |
| J | EDENBRIDGE. Via Gt. Scotland Yard, Kennington, Brixton, Streatham, Norbury, Croydon, Selsdon, Sanderstead, Warlingham, Chelsham, Oxted, Limpsfield | 2 hours 2/- Single 3/- Return |
| J | CHELSHAM Via Great Scotland Yard, Kennington, Brixton, Streatham, Norbury, Croydon, Selsdon, Sanderstead, Warlingham | 30 mins. 1/3 Single 2/- Return |
| L | TUNBRIDGE WELLS. Via Gt. Scotland Yard, Elephant & Castle, New Cross, Lewisham, Catford, Bromley, Farnborough, Green St. Green, Sevenoaks, Hildenborough, Tonbridge, Southborough | 30 mins. 3/6 Single 3/10 Return |
| M | †MAIDENHEAD. Via Shepherds Bush, Youngs Corner, Gt. West Road, Lampton, Cranford, Colnbrook, Slough, Taplow | 30 mins. 2/6 Single 3/6 Return |
| N | †WINDSOR. Via Shepherds Bush, Youngs Corner, Hounslow, Bedfont, Staines, Egham, Englefield Green, Old Windsor | 30 mins. 2/- Single 3/6 Return |
| P | RICKMANSWORTH. Via Harrow Road, Harlesden, Wembley, Sudbury, Harrow-on-the-Hill, Pinner, Northwood, Batchworth Heath | 30 mins. 2/- Single 2/6 Return |

## From GREEN LINE COACH STATION
Poland Street, near Oxford Circus.   Gerrard 2101
### and OXFORD CIRCUS—contd.

| Route Letter | TO | Service Interval and Through Fares |
|---|---|---|
| Q | †UXBRIDGE. Via Shepherds Bush, Acton, Ealing, Hanwell, Southall, Hayes, Hillingdon | Approx. 30 mins. 1/- Single 1/6 Return |
| S | *SUNBURY COMMON. Via Piccadilly, Hammersmith, Richmond, Kingston, Busby Park, Hampton Court, Hampton, Kempton Park | 30 mins. 1/6 Single 2/6 Return |
| U | EAST GRINSTEAD. Via Gt Scotland Yd., Kennington, Brixton, Streatham, Norbury, Croydon, Purley, Kenley, Whyteleafe, Caterham, Godstone, Lingfield | 60 mins. 2/- Single 3/- Return |
| X | SEVENOAKS. Via Gt. Scotland Yard, Elephant & Castle, New Cross, Lewisham, Catford, Bromley, Keston, Biggin Hill, Westerham, Brasted, Sundridge, Riverhead | 60 mins. 2/- Single 3/- Return |
| Y | *WEST BYFLEET (for Woking). Via Shepherds Bush, Hammersmith, Barnes, Roehampton, Kingston-by-pass, Sandown Park, Esher, Cobham, Byfleet (for Brooklands) | 30 mins. 2/- Single 3/- Return |

## From GREAT SCOTLAND YARD
Whitehall
### and PICCADILLY CIRCUS

| Route Letter | TO | Service Interval and Through Fares |
|---|---|---|
| A | *ASCOT. Via Hyde Park Corner, Hammersmith, Youngs Corner, Hounslow, Feltham, Ashford, Staines, Egham, Virginia Water, Blacknest, Sunninghill | 60 mins. 2/6 Return 3/6 Return |
| A | *SUNNINGDALE. Via Hyde Park Corner, Hammersmith, Youngs Corner, Hounslow, Feltham, Ashford, Staines, Egham, Virginia Water | 60 mins. 2/6 Single 3/6 Return |
| A | DARTFORD. Via Elephant & Castle, New Cross, Blackheath, Shooters Hill, Welling, Bexley Heath, Crayford | 30 mins. 1/9 Single 2/3 Return |

## From BISHOPSGATE
(Hamilton House)

| Route Letter | TO | Week-days |
|---|---|---|
| AO | ONGAR. Via Dalston, Leyton, Walthamstow, Chingford, Robin Hood, Epping, North Weald | 20-40 mins. (approx.) Sun. 30 mins 2/- Single 3/- Return |

*Above*: Comprehensive Greenline fare schedule, 1932.

*Opposite*: Greenline Coaches were a subsidiary of London General Omnibus Company – soon to become part of London Transport. Their marketing saw the potential in encouraging love and exploration of London's surrounding countryside.

# GREEN·LINE
# COACH GUIDE FOR RAMBLERS

| Route Letter | Route. | Service Interval & Through Fares. | Route Letter | Route. | Service Interval & Through Fares. |
|---|---|---|---|---|---|
| A | *ASCOT. From Gt. Scotland Yd. (Whitehall). Via Trafalgar Square, Piccadilly, Hyde Park Corner, High St., Kensington, Olympia and Hammersmith. | 60 Mins. 2/6 Sin. 3/6 Ret. | F | ‡HERTFORD. From Green Line Coach Station (Poland St.) Via Oxford Circus, Gt. Portland St., Albany St., Camden Town, Tollington Road, Isledon Road and Finsbury Park. | 30 Mins. 1/6 Sin. 2/6 Ret. |
| A | *SUNNINGDALE. From Gt. Scotland Yd. (Whitehall). Via Trafalgar Square, Piccadilly, Hyde Park Corner, High St., Kensington, Olympia and Hammersmith. | 60 Mins. 2/6 Sin. 3/6 Ret. | G | *GUILDFORD. From Green Line Coach Station (Poland St.) Via Oxford Circus, Wigmore Street, Edgware Road, Hyde Park Street, Bayswater Road, Shepherd's Bush, Holland Road and Hammersmith. | 30 Mins. 2/- Sin. 3/6 Ret. |
| A | DARTFORD. From Gt. Scotland Yd. (Whitehall). Via Westminster Stn., Lambeth North Stn. and Elephant & Castle. | 30 Mins. 1/9 Sin. 2/3 Ret. | H | ‡HARPENDEN. From Oxford Cir. (279 Regent St., W.) Via Portland Place, Baker Street Stn., Finchley Road and Golders Green. | 30 Mins. 2/- Sin. 3/- Ret. |
| B | BRENTWOOD. From Charing Cross (Und. Stn. Emb.) Via Embankment, St. Paul's (Sthn. Rly. Stn.), Mansion House Stn., Cannon Street, Monument, Tower Hill and Aldgate. [Gidea Park—London. Every 7½ mins. rush-hours]. | 15 Mins. 1/6 Sin. 2/6 Ret. | H | GREAT BOOKHAM. From Oxford Cir. (279 Regent St., W.) Via Regent Street, Piccadilly Circus, Charing Cross, Westminster Station, Lambeth North Stn and Kennington. | 30 Mins. 1/6 Sin. 2/6 Ret. |
| C | *CHERTSEY. From Green Line Coach Station (Poland St.) Via Regent Street, Piccadilly, Hyde Park Corner, High St., Kensington, Olympia and Hammersmith. | 30 Mins. 2/3 Sin. 3/6 Ret. | I | FARNINGHAM. From Green Line Coach Station (Poland St.) Via Regent Street, Piccadilly Circus, Charing Cross, Westminster Station, Lambeth North Station and Elephant & Castle. | 60 Mins. 1/9 Sin. 2/9 Ret. |
| D | DORKING. From Green Line Coach Station (Poland St.) Via Regent Street, Piccadilly Circus, Charing Cross, Westminster Station, Lambeth North Station and Kennington. | 30 Mins. 2/- Sin. 3/- Ret. | J | EDENBRIDGE. From Green Line Coach Station (Poland St.) Via Regent Street, Piccadilly Circus, Charing Cross, Westminster Station, Lambeth North Stn. and Kennington. | 120 Mins. 2/- Sin. 3/- Ret. |
| E | BUSHEY. From Oxford Cir. (279 Regent St. W.) Via Wigmore Street, Portman Square, Seymour Street, Edgware Road and Kilburn. | 30 Mins. 1/3 Sin. 1/9 Ret. | J | CHELSHAM. From Green Line Coach Station (Poland St.) Via Regent Street, Piccadilly Circus, Charing Cross, Westminster Station, Lambeth North Stn. and Kennington. | 30 Mins. 1/3 Sin. 2/- Ret. |
| E | REDHILL. From Oxford Cir. (279 Regent St., W.) Via Regent Street, Piccadilly Circus, Charing Cross, Westminster Station, Lambeth North Station and Kennington. | 30 Mins. 2/- Sin. 3/- Ret. | K | HEMEL HEMPSTEAD. From Oxford Cir. (279 Regent St., W.) Via Wigmore Street, Portman Square, Seymour Street, Edgware Road and Kilburn. | 60 Mins. 1/9 Sin. 2/6 Ret. |
| E | CRAWLEY. From Oxford Cir. (279 Regent St., W.) Via Regent Street, Piccadilly Circus, Charing Cross, Westminster Station, Lambeth North Stn. & Kennington. | 60 Mins. 2/6 Sin. 4/- Ret. | K | CATERHAM. From Oxford Cir. (279 Regent St., W.) Via Regent Street, Piccadilly Circus, Charing Cross, Westminster Station, Lambeth North Stn. & Kennington. | 60 Mins. 1/3 Sin. 1/9 Ret. |

Thames Valley Buses parked up in High Wycombe bus station, 1969. The town's distinctive viaduct marks the background. Their post-deregulation successor Wycombe Bus survived for a mere fourteen years, folding in 1990. (Andrew Shouler)

The Thames Valley Traction Company Limited was formed in 1920, merging with Aldershot & District in 1972 to form Alder Valley. These companies were split up in 1986. The former Thames Valley company became the Berks Bucks Bus Company, trading as Beeline.

R. J. Cook: 'I arrived by truck, delivering parts to the site in High Wycombe in 2014. I hadn't seen so many red Routemasters in one place since my London days in the 1970s. Nostalgia for old buses is big business because buses did so much to define and contain working people's freedom to work, socialise and travel. These buses are hired out for special occasions, like weddings.'

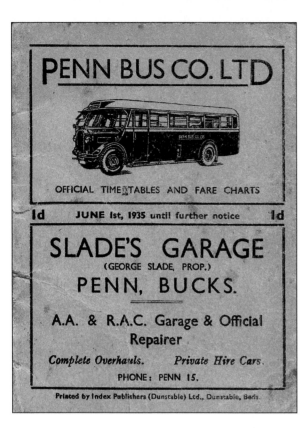

# PENN BUS CO. LTD

OFFICIAL TIMETABLES AND FARE CHARTS

1d   JUNE 1st, 1935 until further notice   1d

## SLADE'S GARAGE
### (GEORGE SLADE, PROP.)
## PENN, BUCKS.

A.A. & R.A.C. Garage & Official Repairer

*Complete Overhauls.*   *Private Hire Cars.*

PHONE: PENN 15.

Printed by Index Publishers (Dunstable) Ltd., Dunstable, Beds.

*Left*: Early bus companies were often a sideline for motor garages, which in turn were inspired by blacksmith shops. Such was the case with the Penn Bus Company. This was its timetable for 1 June 1935.

*Below*: A list of Penn Bus Company's 1935 routes.

# PENN BUS CO. LTD

Registered Office:
### St. John's Rd., Tylers Green, Bucks
Telephone PENN 18

Branch Office: 35 Frogmoor, High Wycombe
Telephone HIGH WYCOMBE 94

*Official*
# TIME TABLES & FARE CHARTS

1d    JUNE 1st, 1935, until further notice    1d

## CONTENTS

| | Page |
|---|---|
| Index to Towns and Villages served | 4—5 |
| List of routes | 1 |
| Passenger regulations | 2—3 |
| Parcels Service | 3 |
| Private Hire | 20 |
| Time tables | 6—17 |
| Fare tables | 19—24 |

### LIST OF ROUTES

| Route No. | Route | Pages Times | Fares |
|---|---|---|---|
| 1 | HIGH WYCOMBE — Hazlemere — PENN | 6—7 | 19 |
| 2 | HIGH WYCOMBE — North Dean — SPEEN | 8 | 19 |
| 3 | TYLERS GREEN — BEACONSFIELD STATION | 8 | 21 |
| 4 | HIGH WYCOMBE — Loudwater — WOOBURN GREEN | 9—11 | 21 |
| 5 | HIGH WYCOMBE — Loudwater — FLACKWELL HEATH | 9—11 | 21 |
| 6 | HIGH WYCOMBE LOCAL, Frogmoor — Mill End Road | 12 | 23 |
| 7 | HIGH WYCOMBE — Prestwood — GT. MISSENDEN | 14—15 | 23 |
| 7A | HIGH WYCOMBE LOCAL, Qn. Victoria Rd.—Crossways | 13 | 23 |
| 8 | HIGH WYCOMBE — TOTTERIDGE | 16 | 24 |
| 9 | HIGH WYCOMBE — WEST WYCOMBE | 17 | 24 |
| 10 | HIGH WYCOMBE — West Wycombe — NAPHILL | 17 | 24 |

PENN]    1

*Right*: Period advertising from 1935.

*Below*: Extract from Penn Bus Company's 1935 timetable.

A.M. TIMES ARE IN LIGHT TYPE.                    P.M. TIMES ARE IN HEAVY TYPE.

## HIGH WYCOMBE (Queen Victoria Road) — LANE END — FRIETH — TURVILLE

| | NS | NS | NS | NS | | FSO | | NS | FSO | SSO | SO | | SO |
|---|---|---|---|---|---|---|---|---|---|---|---|---|---|
| TURVILLE ... | 610 | | | | 9†0 | 1†0 | | 5†0 | | | | | |
| SKIRMETT ... | | | | | 9†5 | 1†5 | | 5†5 | | | | | |
| FINGEST ... | 618 | | | | 9†9 | 1†9 | | 5†9 | | | | | |
| FRIETH ... | 625 | 650 | 7 25 | 8 16 | 9 16 | 1125 1 16 | 1 44 244 344 444 | 5 21 5 51 | 6 34 7 34 7 44 | 8 44 | 9 34 | 9 44 | |
| LANE END ... | 629 | 654 | 7 29 | 8 20 | 9 20 | 1130 1 20 | 1 48 248 348 448 | 5 25 5 55 | 6 38 7 38 7 48 | 8 48 | 9 38 | 9 48 | |
| BOULTER END .. | 632 | 657 | 7 32 | 8 23 | 9 23 | 1133 1 23 | 1 51 251 351 451 | 5 28 5 58 | 6 41 7 41 7 51 | 8 51 | 9 41 | 9 51 | |
| WHEELER END . | 635 | 7 0 | 7 35 | 8 26 | 9 26 | 1136 1 26 | 1 54 254 354 454 | 5 31 6 1 | 6 44 7 44 7 54 | 8 54 | 9 44 | 9 54 | |
| PIDDINGTON ... | 639 | 7 4 | 7 39 | 8 30 | 9 30 | 1140 1 30 | 1 58 258 358 458 | 5 35 6 5 | 6 48 7 48 7 58 | 8 58 | 9 48 | 9 58 | |
| W. WYCOMBE.. | 644 | 7 9 | 7 44 | 8 35 | 9 35 | 1145 1 35 | 2 3 3 3 4 3 5 3 | 5 40 6 10 | 6 53 7 53 8 3 | 9 3 | 9 53 | 10 3 | |
| H. WYCOMBE.. | 654 | 719 | 7 54 | 8 45 | 9 45 | 1152 1 45 | 2 13 313 413 513 | 5 50 6 20 | 7 3 8 3 8 13 | 9 13 | 10 3 | 1013 | |

| | NS | NS | | NS | FSS | | NS | | FO | NS | | SO | | SO | SE | SO |
|---|---|---|---|---|---|---|---|---|---|---|---|---|---|---|---|---|
| H. WYCOMBE | 655 | 755 | 10 5 | 12 0 | 1 47 | 2 15 | 3 15 4 15 515 6 0 | | 6 30 | 7 5 | 8 5 8 15 | 9 15 | 10 5 | 1015 | 1030 | |
| W. WYCOMBE. | 7 5 | 8 5 | 1015 | 12 10 | 1 57 | 2 25 | 3 25 4 25 525 610 | | 6 40 | 7 15 | 8 15 8 25 | 9 25 | 1015 | 1025 | 1040 | |
| PIDDINGTON ... | 710 | 810 | 1020 | 12 15 | 2 2 | 2 30 | 3 30 4 30 530 615 | | 6 45 | 7 20 | 8 20 8 30 | 9 30 | 1020 | 1030 | 1045 | |
| WHEELER END . | 714 | 814 | 1024 | 12 19 | 2 6 | 2 34 | 3 34 4 34 534 619 | | 6 49 | 7 24 | 8 24 8 34 | 9 34 | 1024 | 1034 | 1049 | |
| BOULTER END . | 717 | 817 | 1027 | 12 22 | 2 9 | 2 37 | 3 37 4 37 537 622 | | 6 52 | 7 27 | 8 27 8 37 | 9 37 | 1027 | 1037 | 1052 | |
| LANE END ... | 720 | 820 | 1030 | 12 25 | 2 12 | 2 40 | 3 40 4 40 540 625 | | 6 55 | 7 30 | 8 30 8 40 | 9 40 | 1030 | 1040 | 1055 | |
| FRIETH ... | 724 | 824 | 1034 | 12 29 | 2 16 | 2 44 | 3 44 4 44 544 629 | 629 | 6 59 | 7 34 | 8 34 8 44 | 9 44 | 1034 | 1044 | 1059 | |
| FINGEST ... | | | | 12†35 | | | 4†50 | | 633 | 7* 3 | 8 41 | | 1041 | | | |
| SKIRMETT ... | | | | 12†39 | | | 4†54 | | 637 | 7* 7 | 8 45 | | 1045 | | | |
| TURVILLE ... | | | | 12†44 | | | 4†59 | | 641 | 7*11 | 8 50 | | 1050 | | | |

NS—Not Sunday.   SO—Saturday only.   SSO—Saturday and Sunday only.   SE—Saturday excepted.
FSO or †—Friday and Saturday only.   *—Not Friday and Saturday.   FO—Friday only.
FSS—Friday Saturday and Sunday only.

On Bank Holidays, First buses will be as on Sundays, but full Saturday service will operate throughout the day.

On Boxing Day, Sunday service will operate.   No service on Christmas Day.

# 5

# Uniting Counties

Thomas Tilling ran their first motor bus in 1904, starting with horse buses in London, but growth was frustrated by the London General Omnibus Company's monopoly. British Electric Traction (BET) were next with a London motor bus. They operated through a subsidiary – British Automobile Traction Co Ltd (BAT). The two companies formed TBAT in May 1928.

The London Transport Passenger Board took over all London Transport in 1934, forcing TBAT to grow elsewhere. Meanwhile, a bus crew working for the London Central Omnibus Company were running a weekend sideline around their home town using a company bus. It was profitable but got them sacked. Still, they had enough money to buy their own bus, and founded the Wellingborough Motor Bus Company in May 1913.

The company blossomed into the United Counties Road Transport Company, registered on 1 September 1921. Tilling spotted a bargain after buying Eastern National, exploiting the poor rail services out of East London. BET were already running Peterborough trams. A national system was the way forward. United Counties Omnibus Company was officially registered when Tilling bought the company in 1933, but it would wait until 1952 before Tilling designated this subsidiary to its long-running hegemony in North Bucks, ending only with deregulation.

Tilling's Bristol Commercial Vehicle and ECW bus bodybuilding subsidiaries brought uniformity to the area, extended to Thames Valley by the same process, with services running from High Wycombe into Aylesbury. By 1927, Thames Valley had standardised on Tilling Stevens' petrol-driven buses. At this time BAT owned 86 per cent of Thames Valley Traction shares, with Tilling owning the other 12 per cent.

BAT was reconstituted as Tilling & British Automobile Traction Ltd in 1928. Thames Valley expanded significantly in the 1920s and 1930s by buying a number of smaller firms and their routes. In 1948, Tilling sold out to the British Transport Commission, thus becoming a nationalised company. Thames Valley's expansion continued in the early 1950s. Other parts of the newly nationalised bus network were put under Thames Valley management, such as South Midland and Newbury & District from Red and White Bus Services and part of UCOC.

City of Oxford Motor Services (COMS) were a familiar sight in and around Aylesbury, with services running west to Thame, Oxford (only 20 miles away), Bicester and Fringford.

COMS had started life running trams and horse buses. The company replaced these with Daimler motor buses in 1913–14. They reformed as City of Oxford Motor Services in 1921. BET took them over in the 1930s along with other bus operators.

The Great Western Railway entered Oxford in the 1840s and took a minority shareholding in COMS. BET favoured AEC vehicles built at Southall, leading to a prevalence of Regals and Regents alongside Tilling's (in-house-built) Bristols. The fleet livery was red with maroon and pale green relief.

Transport Minister Barbara Castle made 1968 a big year, with new legislation forcing nationalisation. So, Tilling's main competitor, BET, sold its bus interests to the Transport Holding Company (successor to the BTC) and the Transport Act 1968 formed the National Bus Company, which came into existence on 1 January 1969, amalgamating the interests of the Tilling Group with the recently acquired BET Group.

COMS became a subsidiary of the National Bus Company in 1969. Sadly, that was the end of the distinctively smart livery. Greater integration of city and country services began. In 1971, the Oxford–London coach operator South Midland, which had been controlled by the neighbouring Thames Valley Traction, was transferred to COMS, and the fleet name for the entire operation became Oxford South Midland. AEC vehicles began to fade out in favour of Bristol VRs. These were more suitable to one-man operated buses (OMO), cutting costs and dealing with labour shortages. United Counties, Red Rover and the whole country were following the same path.

Aylesbury's lively, colourful Kingsbury Square had by then given way to the Friars Square terminus. For a couple of years there were still the odd and characteristic bus crews, with conductors having money bags and whirling ticket machines held over their shoulders by leather straps. Drivers wore their little red and white circle numbered badges; the conductors had a green rim. Tea and snacks were served in a corner of the bus station, which is now a rather dirty loading and parking area.

A Bristol LWL6B United Counties single-decker roaming the lanes near the Bucks–Northants county border, c. 1956. (John Royle)

UCOC's fleet number 910, a KSW6B still shiningly new in 1953, about to work the long winding route from Oxford to Bedford in 1953. In those bygone days Crosse & Blackwell are seen advertising 'Beans for the Boys' – a slogan that wouldn't be seen today.

| LIGHT FIGURES DENOTE A.M. TIMES | | | | | | | | | | DARK FIGURES DENOTE P.M. TIMES | | | | |
|---|---|---|---|---|---|---|---|---|---|---|---|---|---|---|

**131**  BEDFORD — WOLVERTON — BUCKINGHAM — OXFORD  **131**
Joint Service by United Counties Omnibus Co. Ltd. and City of Oxford Motor Services Ltd.

FOR ADDITIONAL TIMES BETWEEN : Bedford and Bromham, see Services 115, 128, 130, 132, 133 ; Bedford and Lavendon, see Service 127 ; Stony Stratford and New Bradwell, see Service 391 (Western Area Timetable)

No passenger may be taken up, at or between Stony Stratford, Wolverton and New Bradwell for the purpose of being set down at or between those places in either direction.

|  | WEEKDAYS | | | | SUNDAYS | | | |  | WEEKDAYS | | | | SUNDAYS | |
|---|---|---|---|---|---|---|---|---|---|---|---|---|---|---|---|
|  | UC | OXF | UC | OXF | | | | |  | OXF | UC | OXF | UC | OXF | UC |
| Bedford, Omnibus Station | 7 20 | 1115 | 2 30 | 5 55 | 2 30 | 6 30 | | | Oxford, Gloucester Green | 7 50 | 1050 | 2 15 | 5 50 | 2 15 | 6 15 |
| Bedford, Midland Road Rly. Station | 7 25 | 1120 | 2 35 | 6 0 | 2 35 | 6 35 | | | Gosford, King's Arms | 8 5 | 11 5 | 2 30 | 6 5 | 2 30 | 6 30 |
| Bromham, The Swan | 7 35 | 1130 | 2 45 | 6 10 | 2 45 | 6 45 | | | Wendlebury, Red Lion | 8 20 | 1120 | 2 45 | 6 20 | 2 45 | 6 45 |
| Turvey, Schools | C7*46 | 1141 | 2 56 | 6 21 | 2 56 | 6 56 | | | Bicester, Market Place | 8 27 | 1127 | 2 52 | 6 27 | 2 52 | 6 52 |
| Olney, The Bull | C8 8 | 1153 | 3 8 | 6 33 | 3 8 | 7 8 | | | Finmere Railway Station | B8 45 | 1145 | 3 10 | 6 45 | 3 10 | 7 10 |
| Emberton, The Bell | 8 11 | 1156 | 3 11 | 6 36 | 3 11 | 7 11 | | | Tingewick, Royal Oak | B 51 | 1151 | 3 16 | 6 51 | 3 16 | 7 16 |
| Sherington, The Swan | 8 16 | 12 1 | 3 16 | 6 41 | 3 16 | 7 16 | | | Buckingham, Town Hall { arr. | 9 0 | 12 0 | 3 25 | 7 0 | 3 25 | 7 25 |
| Newport Pagnell, Market Hill | 8 21 | 12 6 | 3 21 | 6 46 | 3 21 | 7 21 | | | { dep. | 9 5 | 12 5 | 3 30 | 7 5 | 3 30 | 7 30 |
| New Bradwell, Foresters Arms | C8 31 | 1216 | 3 31 | 6 56 | 3 31 | 7 31 | | | Leckhampstead Turn | 9 11 | 1211 | 3 36 | 7 11 | 3 36 | 7 36 |
| Wolverton, North Western Hotel | B8 36 | 1221 | 3 36 | 7 1 | 3 36 | 7 36 | | | Deanshanger, The Beehive | 9 19 | 1219 | 3 44 | 7 19 | 3 44 | 7 44 |
| Stony Stratford, Wolverton Road | 8 41 | 1226 | 3 41 | 7 6 | 3 41 | 7 41 | | | Old Stratford, The Swan | 9 24 | 1224 | 3 49 | 7 24 | 3 49 | 7 49 |
| Old Stratford, The Swan | 8 46 | 1231 | 3 46 | 7 11 | 3 46 | 7 46 | | | Stony Stratford, Wolverton Road | 9 29 | 1229 | 3 54 | 7 29 | 3 54 | 7 54 |
| Deanshanger, The Beehive | 8 51 | 1236 | 3 51 | 7 16 | 3 51 | 7 51 | | | Wolverton, opp. N. Western Hotel | B9 34 | 1234 | 3 59 | 7 34 | 3 59 | 7 59 |
| Leckhampstead Turn | 8 59 | 1244 | 3 59 | 7 24 | 3 59 | 7 59 | | | New Bradwell, Foresters Arms | C9 39 | 1239 | 4 4 | 7 39 | 4 4 | |
| Buckingham, Town Hall { arr. | 9 5 | 1250 | 4 5 | 7 30 | 4 5 | 8 5 | | | Newport Pagnell, Market Hill | 9 49 | 1249 | 4 14 | 7 49 | 4 14 | 8 14 |
| { dep. | 9 10 | 1255 | 4 10 | 7 35 | 4 10 | 8 10 | | | Sherington, The Swan | 9 54 | 1254 | 4 19 | 7 54 | 4 19 | 8 19 |
| Tingewick, Royal Oak | 9 19 | 1 4 | 4 19 | 7 44 | 4 19 | 8 19 | | | Emberton, The Bell | 9 59 | 1259 | 4 24 | 7 59 | 4 24 | 8 24 |
| Finmere, Railway Station | B9 25 | 1 10 | 4 25 | 7 50 | 4 25 | 8 25 | | | Olney, The Bull | C10 2 | 1 2 | 4 27 | 8 2 | 4 27 | 8 27 |
| Bicester, Market Place | 9 43 | 1 28 | 4 43 | 8 8 | 4 43 | 8 43 | | | Turvey, Schools | C10 14 | 1 14 | 4 39 | 8 14 | 4 39 | 8 39 |
| Wendlebury, Red Lion | 9 50 | 1 35 | 4 50 | 8 15 | 4 50 | 8 50 | | | Bromham, The Swan | 1025 | 1 25 | 4 50 | 8 25 | 4 50 | 8 50 |
| Gosford, King's Arms | 10 5 | 1 50 | 5 5 | 8 30 | 5 5 | 9 5 | | | Bedford, Midland Road Rly. Station | 1035 | 1 35 | 5 0 | 8 35 | 5 0 | 9 0 |
| Oxford, Gloucester Green | 1020 | 2 5 | 5 20 | 8 45 | 5 20 | 9 20 | | | Bedford, Omnibus Station | 1040 | 1 40 | 5 5 | 8 40 | 5 5 | 9 5 |

*—Calls Lavendon (Cross) 7.51 a.m.    B—Buses stop adjacent to Railway Station.    C—Buses stop within 300 yards of Railway Station.    OXF—Operated by City of Oxford.
UC—Operated by United Counties.

INTERAVAILABILITY OF ROAD AND RAIL TICKETS exists on this route as between Oxford and Bicester, see page 27

**TRAVEL BY ROAD AND SEE THE COUNTRY**

The 1950s 131 timetable, showing how challenging a run it was for the crew of a lumbering Bristol K type.

Eastern National's Western operational area, from the cover of their 1952 timetable. (Colin Harvey Taylor)

Market Square, Newport Pagnell, 11 May 1972. This ex-Birch UCOC Leyland Leopard coach is on service 324 and will return to Bletchley. (A. Shouler)

This UCOC Bristol KSW6B was new in 1953 – fleet number 934. It stands ready with the Buckingham service. Red Rover's timetable is attached to the wall, just in front of the bus. (R. H. G. Simpson)

Cover detail from the March 1953 United Counties timetable. It shows the eastern and western operational areas of the company following Tilling's reorganisation. (Colin Harvey Taylor)

*Above*: Kingsbury Square. This single-deck Bristol L5G (5 and G were references to cylinder and Gardner engines as opposed to B for Bristol power units) was new to Eastern National in 1938, passing to UCOC on May 1952, then withdrawn in 1956. It stands next to the UCOC Luton service, with London Transport 's 359 RT service to Little Missenden in the background. (R. H. G. Simpson)

*Below*: Photographed at 8.40 a.m. on Saturday 20 July 1985 on Market Hill, Newport Pagnell. York Bros bought Wesleys in 1979 but retained their livery. It prepares to leave on service 526. The UCOC Leyland National 556 passes by on the 425 service to Penny Lodge before returning at 9 a.m. to Bletchley via Central Milton Keynes. It advertises 'City Rider' tickets – £4.40 per week and £16.50 per month. (Andrew Shouler)

*Above*: United Counties express coach in new National Express colours, heading from Newport Pagnell to the M1 in 1971. (Andrew Shouler)

*Below*: An inspector waits to board OND79 in Wolverton, en route to New Bradwell, in the early 1970s.

Former London Transport RT 61, Red Rover's second RT parked in Buckingham's Market Square bus turnaround, *c.* 1958. The ivy-clad Old Gaol makes an idyllic backdrop. Red Rover ran a joint service backwards and forwards to Aylesbury with UCOC. (R. H. G. Simpson)

# 6

# Country Ways

Robert Cook noted in *The Red Rover Story*:

> It was remarkable that a busy market town like Aylesbury had only one independent bus operator. That company changed considerably from the 1960s until takeover by Luton & District. This was an age of hope for the buses.
>
> When the Great Central's rail services to Calvert were cut and the Oxford–Cambridge passenger line closed, Red Rover took the commercial initiative organising rail replacement services. A three month trial became permanent, for which Red Rover's first AEC Swift, registration XBH55F was ideally suited. A Brackley service began when the Great Central Line closed down permanently in 1966. At first a stage route as far as Edgcott, it became an express connection.
>
> Swifts and Reliances were further shifts to one man operation and RTs disappeared from all routes in 1968. South Wales provided a Regent in name, but hardly the same as an RT. Devon General also provided another Mark V Regent in the same years.
>
> Leyland Leopards became the shape of the 1970s, offering luxury coach comfort on stage routes, including music when certain drivers were in control. Government legislation favoured one man buses for subsidy.

The company went on to purchase three Plaxton Supreme Five express coaches, built on Leyland Tiger chassis. They had fifty-five reclining seats, ideally suited for the dual purpose of Keith Coaches' excursion and contract work, but still qualifying for the 50 per cent government subsidy for rural operations.

Coach excursions were a development from the age of charabanc outings in the 1920s. Affectionately known as 'charas', these vehicles were like giant open-top touring cars with fold-away hoods. The most popular destinations were to the seaside. Closer to home, a day touring the Chilterns, stopping at a country pub and for a good walk, was a holiday for many.

Against this background, a plethora of Buckinghamshire coach operators set up business, usually as an offshoot of a garage business, as with Bill French and his Winslow Coaches.

Classic Coaches Bristol RE on heritage services, crossing Granborough Brook, September 1995. Robert Cook recalls these coaches operating for Eastern Counties (the Cheltenham–Norwich–Great Yarmouth express service through Buckingham). He caught it during his undergraduate years at the University of East Anglia in the early 1970s. Robert said, 'As we get older, we look back on emblems and symbols of our youth. Naturally we would like to go back and do it all better, meet people we took for granted and lost. Being young was more hopeful and romantic then.'

Winslow's Red Cross Club enjoying a day out at Ashgrove Gardens. The coach was hired from Red Rover, with renowned driver 'General' Clarke standing on the left.

Red Rover driver 'General' Clarke was at the wheel of this utility-bodied Daimler double-decker when the wind blew it over at the top of Oving Hill in winter 1947. (*Bucks Herald*)

One of Grendon's Raisey's coaches stops over at the much-loved Busy Bee Cafe on the A41, returning from a day trip back from London in 1959. (George Tasker)

Keith Garages in Bicester Road, home to Keith Coaches, newly opened in 1930 by Stuart Mills's father. Far-sighted Stuart drove the business forward, buying Red Rover Omnibus Company from E. M. Cain in 1955. Cain's garage was located near the Elmhurst traffic lights and became a car sales outlet. It is a vacant site at time of writing. Keith Coaches, Red Rover and Keith Coaches are no more. (Stuart Mills)

Ironmonger and general supply retailer F. R. Markham at work in his Buckingham office in the late 1970s. The large National Express coach model was a symbol of his successful coach agency sideline for Eastern Counties, Black & White and then National Express, which absorbed both companies.

# PRIVATE HIRE SERVICE

## WE WILL —

★ SUBMIT QUOTATIONS TO SUIT THE INDIVI-
  DUAL REQUIREMENTS OF YOUR PARTY
★ PROVIDE NEW SUPER-LUXURY COACHES
★ SUGGEST ATTRACTIVE ITINERARIES AND
  PLACES OF INTEREST AND AMUSEMENT IF
  DESIRED
★ BOOK SEATS FOR THEATRES, PANTOMIME,
  SPORTING EVENTS, etc.
★ RELIEVE YOU OF ANXIETY AS TO YOUR
  TRAVEL ARRANGEMENTS

OUR LONG EXPERIENCE IN CATERING FOR PRIVATE
PARTY TRAVEL IS AT YOUR DISPOSAL, AND WILL HELP
TO MAKE YOUR OUTING A PLEASANT EXPERIENCE AND
A SUCCESS

*Right*: Another page that speaks of a long-lost age. UCOC advertise their coach hire services in the late 1940s.

*Below*: Soul's six-wheeler parked outside Church House in July 1971. Back in the 1930s, this company was trading as R. Souls of Olney, becoming the butt of many a schoolboy's joke. (Andrew Shouler)

Todd's Coaches, based at Whitchurch Garage, were another North Bucks stalwart running excursions and school. This one, pictured in the mid-1950s, was on hire to UCOC. (R. H. G. Simpson)

George Tasker, of Langston & Tasker, encountering busy holiday traffic on an excursion from Steeple Claydon in the late 1950s. (George Tasker)

Robert Cook recalls his first outing on French's snub-nosed Bedford OB cream, lime and bottle green coach heading eastward to Great Yarmouth:

I was only about four years old. It was organised by Nin and Frank Warner, who ran the Nag's Head pub in Sheep Street, Winslow just up the road from us. It was very exciting. Up at 4 in the morning, having my cornflakes and off we went. My sister was complaining that she would rather still be in bed. But I loved buses and lorries.

We had to start early because it was a long way – 148 miles. I remember all the beer crates being loaded from the pub by young Bill French and Frank Warner. I didn't know why men liked beer so much.

When we got to Yarmouth it was misty. I saw a ship's funnel peeking through. We went to the amusement arcade where there was a frightening lifelike puppet in a big glass box. It was called the Laughing Policeman. When my mum put a penny in it started moving, singing along to turgid music, gyrating and laughing. I thought it was horrible.

The weather brightened. We were friends with the Warners and their son Tony. So, while our hard-working parents rested, dads on the beer, Tony and I started building sandcastles. Then when our parents were drifting away in their deckchairs and my sister reposing on the sand, we rushed down into the sea. Luckily someone saw us before we were swept away. Our clothes had to be dried in the sunshine.

A lot of the people on the coach had been to the pub, then drank what was left in the coach's boot on the long way back. As if that was not enough, we stopped off at a big pub in Newmarket. Then I fell asleep until carried out into the darkness and down the road to our little house. It had been a magical day. Pleasures were simple in those days.

This was a tragic accident in Granborough in the early 1930s. A Red Rover driver swerved to avoid a child but collided with a house which killed a baby inside.

*Above*: Robinson's Coaches of Stewkley, November 1994. This is another long-gone Buckinghamshire coach business. Robinson's bought Red Rover's second AEC Bridgemaster (6116BH), a diverted Scottish order for a very unpopular type.

*Left*: This advertisement from Bletchley's Buckmasters, *c.* 1957, is another blast from the past.

Dennis Mauger left Red Rover to work for City of Oxford Motor Services, but did part-time excursion driving for his old love, Red Rover. Here he is with his Red Rover's Keith Coach in Bournemouth in the mid-1970s. (Dennis Mauger)

*Above*: Langston & Tasker Buckingham Bull Ring, March 1994. On a local run back home to Steeple Claydon, the well-presented coach carries a rare Ford badge. Jeff's Brackley service is lined up behind. Jeff's took over local firm Payne's Coaches. Payne's depot was through a very narrow archway just right of this view.

*Below*: Prestwood Travel is a thriving operator based near Great Missenden. This vehicle from their 1979 fleet is a fine example of their high standards. It is interesting how small driving mirrors used to be. (Andrew Shouler Collection)

*Above*: This Leyland Olympian leaving Buckingham in May 1994, with ECW body, was new to UCOC in January 1982. It was the penultimate of a group of twenty dating from August 1981. Aylesbury UCOC garage was a sub-depot of Luton. Deregulation triggered a management buyout, creating Luton & District. The Aylesbury allocation wore the Aylesbury Bus name. Following their takeover of Red Rover some local vehicles carried, rather unconvincingly, the Red Rover banner. Stuart Mills, then Red Rover MD, told Robert Cook that Luton's offer was too good to refuse – see *The Red Rover Story* by Robert Cook.

*Below*: Soul's depot in Lime Street, Olney, in the late 1960s, before their move to Yardley Road. (Andrew Shouler)

The county namesake town of Buckingham had two private coach operators, Payne's and A. Varney. The latter was a small and primitive enterprise, but young Mr Varney was an enigmatic character much appreciated around town.

Payne's Coaches, based beside the Bull Ring, was a more substantial and ambitious enterprise. As with Winslow Coaches, it was a marvel to watch the drivers move the ever-larger coaches through the small arch beside the Masonic hall. When the proprietor died, his daughter decided it was best to sell to larger rival Jeff's Coaches.

New safety rules did not favour bus garages in high-density population areas. Payne's had a fire in this garage back in February 1959. Fred Douglas heard the first explosion from his neighbouring cottage where he was watching television. The glow could be seen for miles around but only one coach was scorched.

Another established Bucks coach firm, Dickson's of Stoke Mandeville, sold out to Mott's. The age of small operators was over. Soul's had long abandoned the 'R' at the start of their company name, for obvious reasons, and moved to larger premises. Z&S suddenly appeared on the scene in the 1990s. Its founder started in haulage with one lorry. The company now runs several efficient bus services, including Winslow–Milton Keynes via Bletchley.

Langston & Tasker always had a lot of room by the green in Steeple Claydon. Like Mott's, they have prospered from carrying schoolchildren to ever-larger schools, justifying the purchase of double-deckers. This is how the firm made up for losing the trade of carrying workers to the local brickworks after it closed. The firm originated when Ron Langston and George Tasker married the daughters of a soon to retire local coach operator and were invited to take over the firm.

Dennis Mauger recalls Red Rover as the best of times. He told Robert Cook:

Someone would always talk to you. Red Rover were the best days of my life. Mick Hayward followed his dad into Red Rover and was in charge of bus engineering. When Luton & District took over and I had gone back to work for them at Aylesbury Bus, he became my boss. He said to me 'What is the most important thing on that bus?' The answer was 'a loose nut'. Funny how things turned out. I left Red Rover to get a pension, and I ended up back with them when Aylesbury Bus took over Red Rover.

# 7

# Off the Buses

In the good old days buses were a social world on wheels, with no worry about catching colds or Covid-19. Crucial during the war with special services to facilities like RAF Halton and the Firs munitions factory at Whitchurch, buses were especially busy on local market days and weekend hospital visiting.

The pace was slow. Chirpy conductors were weighed down by leather satchels heavy with money and there were handle-wound ticket machines with mechanisms for printing off strings of differently priced stage tickets. Keeping passengers safe, conductors alone rang the bell. Their shouts of 'room for two more on top' were a relief to the last two in the queue. On top was where the smokers and young lovers sat on the last night ride home. In the morning Red Rover offered a cheap workman's return.

Between 1982 and 1990 bus use fell before starting to increase until 2007/8, when it remained relatively stable until 2014/15, with it falling since then.

Post-war National Bus Company rationalisation created two major groups, Tilling and British Automobile Traction (BAT).

The Second World War took its toll on transport infrastructure, accelerating National Bus Company development, which also worked in harmony with small private operators like Red Rover.

Bucks became a target for post-war London overspill, reaching its peak with the new city (though not legally a city) in the 1970s. Milton Keynes' first turf was cut in 1968. It was planned around grid roads, becoming famous as the 'city of the motor car'.

Over the post-war years, Buckinghamshire lost a large area around Slough and Milton Keynes became a unitary authority.

Following the Labour Party victory at the 1966 general election, Barbara Castle was appointed Minister for Transport. Castle immediately ordered a review of public transport, with a view to formulating a new transport policy. Among the issues to be tackled were the ownership and operation of bus services, which were rapidly losing patronage and profitability due to the increased prevalence of private motor cars. The state owned a considerable proportion of scheduled bus operators outside the major cities, having obtained the Tilling Group companies in 1948 as a by-product of nationalising the railways.

The Tilling Group was subsequently placed under the ownership of the nationalised Transport Holding Company (THC). London Transport was also nationalised in 1948 and others voluntarily acquiesced, the last being Red & White in 1950. When the Labour Party suddenly lost power to the Conservatives in 1951, the nationalisation programme remained unfinished.

Castle proposed forming regional transport authorities, which would take over the THC subsidiaries and municipal transport undertakings in their area, and would also have the power to acquire private bus operators. However, in November 1967 British Electric Traction (BET) unexpectedly offered to sell its bus operations to the government. BET, who had been the only major private bus operating group, received £35 million for its twenty-five provincial bus companies and 11,300 vehicles. The deal meant that the state or municipal bus operators now operated some 90 per cent of scheduled bus services in England and Wales. Instead of forming the regional authorities, the government published a white paper proposing the merger of the THC and BET organisations into a single National Bus Company.

The recommendations of the white paper formed part of the Transport Act 1968. This also reorganised the already nationalised bus operation in Scotland, where subsidiaries formed the Scottish Bus Group.

The National Bus Company was formed on 1 January 1969. In 1970, the company was enlarged when it acquired the country area buses of London Transport (as London Country Bus Services). The new name 'London Country' appeared on the green buses operating from Amersham garage.

Buses were operated by locally managed subsidiary companies with their own fleet names and liveries. In the early years of the company there was some rationalisation, generally leading to the amalgamation of operators into larger units and the transfer of areas between them. One was the merging of Aldershot & District with Thames Valley on 1 January 1972.

Following the appointment of Fred Wood as chairman in 1972, NBC introduced corporate images. Henceforth, its coaches were branded as National Travel and painted in unrelieved white, with the NBC logo and the 'NATIONAL' name in alternate red and blue letters.

The services were rebranded as National Express soon afterwards. The addition of blue and white stripes appeared in 1978. National Travel was the country's first attempt at a uniformly marketable express network, which superseded Associated Motorways and the plethora of other services provided by individual NBC subsidiaries. The coaches were managed by a few areas and included travel agent booking offices based at major bus stations.

A hub and spoke system operated, with the main hub at Cheltenham (although this did not serve the north of England very well). The names Black & White and Eastern Counties had been a daily sight in Buckingham, serving the Cheltenham to Yarmouth service. These liveries were quickly replaced by a new fleet of Leyland Leopards in all white, except for the red and white lettering. It was a five-hour run from Buckingham to Norwich, diverting through Thetford Forest where *Dad's Army* was filmed.

Around the same time the company launched a wide number of UK holiday services under the banner 'National Holidays'. This brand and its travel agent booking offices existed until the mid-1990s, when the coach holiday division closed. UCOC ran a busy office in Aylesbury.

The National Express overseas travel business was relaunched under the name Eurolines. They operated services from the UK across Europe and passengers booked through the main National Express website.

In the 1970s all local service buses adopted a uniform design, generally in either leaf green or poppy red, initially with white relief, and bearing the company fleet name in white with the new NBC double-N arrow logo. There were exceptions to this, but not in Buckinghamshire.

The NBC inherited from the Transport Holding Company 75 per cent shareholdings in chassis manufacturer Bristol Commercial Vehicles and bodybuilder Eastern Coach Works. In 1969, NBC formed a joint venture with British Leyland (who owned the other 25 per cent of Bristol and ECW), by means of which British Leyland became a 50 per cent owner of the NBC's manufacturing companies.

The joint venture designed and built a new single-deck bus, the Leyland National. The first was delivered in 1972 and it remained in production until 1986. The National was also available to other bus operators.

In 1982, NBC sold its 50 per cent interest in the joint venture (including Bristol and ECW) to British Leyland.

Deregulation was expected to promote bus travel. Buckingham had lost its Black & White Eastern Counties express Cheltenham–Yarmouth service through Buckingham. A ticket bought going from Buckingham to Norwich cost £1.50 in 1971. Cheltenham's famous interchange was demolished in the 1980s. Coaches now terminated at Oxford and Cambridge, and were then cut back to Bedford. Bus replacements for the closed-down Oxford–Cambridge line were short-lived.

In 1991, local businessmen organised protests against the closure of the daily Buckingham–London express coach, describing National's decision as another nail in the town's coffin.

There was a steady improvement in coach services. The *Buckingham Advertiser* reported on 15 April 1994:

Public transport was given a boost this week with the launch of improved services for Buckingham, Brackley and Bicester. To mark the occasion, free rides are being offered on a new weekday service from Oxford to Bicester and Buckingham. United Counties and Coachlinks promise speedier journeys and extra services linking three towns with Oxford in response to public demand. And because the number of passengers between Bicester and Oxford has been increasing, fares have not had to rise for nearly two years. Said Coachlinks' Oxfordshire manager, Rod Davies: 'We've been listening to our existing customers and potential passengers.'

Extra journeys are now being operated between Buckingham and Oxford and to meet many requests, a new service will leave Oxford at 5.10 pm on Mondays and Fridays for Bicester and Buckingham. As a special introductory offer, no fares will be charged on this journey until April 25th. This service does not go to Brackley.

A coach leaving Oxford for Bicester has been speeded up to get passengers home earlier.

'An added improvement takes some coaches through to Leicester and Nottingham. Local passengers would be welcome on these services,' said Mr Davies.

A weekly ticket on the popular Oxford to Bicester route is £9 for adults or £5 for children and students.

Arriva were a breath of fresh air on the local scene, ready to adapt to what people wanted. The *Bucks Herald* announced on 10 February 1999:

> Bus users in Princess Risborough should get all the information they need this week to use a new service round the town. Town councillors had praised the introduction of the 325 bus, linking the town, housing estates and railway, but called for the service to be better advertised to encourage Risborughians to use the service. Following an article in last week's Bucks Herald, Arriva the Shires, which operates the service, will tomorrow (Thursday) launch a promotion campaign by handing out leaflets at the town's Charter Market. Timetables are available on 325 buses at the railway station and at the information centre and library.
>
> Nigel Eggleton, Arriva the Shires' commercial director, said: 'New route 325 provides a useful shopping and railway link for Princes Risborough. To encourage as many people as possible to give it a try, Arriva is more than happy to mail the timetable leaflet completely free of charge.

People have taken buses for granted, expecting them to always be there when the car breaks down. This is the age of urban bus lanes, but it needs more than that to get people out of cars and on the buses. There have been many obstacles to the creation of affordable and attractive bus systems in increasingly congested Britain.

Back in February 1995, the government decided to enforce a ban on coaches using the outside lane of motorways with three or more lanes. The move was to make motorways safer, but express coach companies argued that this would create slower journey times and higher fares.

Graham Smith of Heyfordian Travel commented that if a coach is trailing two trucks slowly, overtaking this would slow coach times every time it happened. He said it could create the need for two drivers because of driving hours. Andy Price of Langston & Takser said the ban could result in convoys of coaches. He said that you go as fast as conditions allow and that coach travel was still very safe.

Buckinghamshire has three motorways cutting through it, the M1, M25 and M40, all being very vulnerable to gridlock. Bank holidays are the worst time for this, with well over 15 million cars on the road at the same time. A recent solution has been to convert the hard shoulders to carriageways, leading to a worrying rise in casualties, fatalities and more hold ups. People have become used to gridlock.

With more people driving these days, bus operators are challenged in this environment. The situation in London is rather different because driving is more difficult here due to heavy traffic, and parking even more so. However, even London Transport struggles and often fails to cope because infrastructure cannot keep pace. Buckinghamshire merges with Greater London in the Denham M25 region, where bus transport is on a different level.

South Bucks travellers typically either use the train or have reserved London parking. However, more generally, travelling from the county can be difficult, but entrepreneurs have never lacked ideas. Bucks County Council have been as supportive as local taxes will allow. Bucks initiatives have been plenty, including Travelwise and the Sunday Rover. Dial-a-bus and Community Bus were two further ideas. Milton Keynes City Bus was another initiative, with small Mercedes vehicles and multiple payment methods. Smaller vehicles were seen as a solution for access to estates and reducing fuel costs. Despite these many efforts to encourage bus use, dependence on the motor car is massive.

Ed Grimsdale, retired deputy head teacher at Buckingham's Royal Latin School informed his local paper on 14 July 2000:

> May I carp at your coverage of 'the car' in last week's issue. Pages 2, 3, and 7 were dedicated to the false god. Rob Gibbard, the editor, looks forward to a brave new world of better public transport, local shops and a cleaner environment with fewer cars. He laments it won't happen overnight.
>
> Rob, it will never happen unless folk feel they must partially abandon their cars. Price hikes are painful because habits of a lifetime are broken. The country won't receive neighbourhood shops, a better environment and fewer cars as manna from heaven; but changes may be effected.
>
> In harsh times, substitution is available to all consumers. Out go cars in come bikes and shanks's pony. Suddenly the neighbourhood is alive.

Life for local councils and planners is difficult because transport investment has never been given the priority it deserves.

Council plans to sell off the marble-clad Milton Keynes bus station made local front page news on 13 February 2000. The government appointed the quango English Partnership headed by former British Railways boss Sir Bob Reid, which approached the council with a view to buying the freehold. The bus station had never been fit for purpose, being windswept and bleak, with express coaches diverted to the city centre and Coach Way, just off the M1, near Newport Pagnell. Local buses were accommodated near a shopping centre extension and parking areas adjacent to the rail station.

The following week, *Milton Keynes on Sunday* confirmed reports that the council were selling the bus station and Winterhill depot 'at a massive loss in a bid to get its hands on the cash quickly'. The report continued:

> The authority needs the £2 million proceeds by April to help balance the books for this year's budget. It is also in line for a percentage of the money generated by the development of the sites. But critics say the sale to English Partnership will see the council lose millions on the lucrative sites at Elder Gate and Winterhill.
>
> The council's policy committee approved the go-ahead for the sale at a secret meeting on Tuesday.
>
> English Partnership refused this week to reveal if a developer was interested in the deal, claiming it wanted to buy the freehold of the properties which it leases from the council 'just in case.'
>
> Liberal Democrats say the Labour plan to sell the sites is a way of making a quick buck. Liberal leader Irene Henderson said: 'They need this money as quickly as they can get it to plug the hole in the budget. The sites are worth a lot more than the amount being paid for them but they have accepted a lesser deal to get the money quickly.'

An independent property valuer contacted by Milton Keynes on Sunday said the two sites, with planning permission for commercial development would be worth up to £10 million.

The council needs the cash to help pay off some of the £5 million overspend on the new theatre and gallery. A million and a half of the overspend must be paid off this year.

The council had acted as guarantor for the multi-million-pound project, with the taxpayer lined up to pay the bill. A report to the finance committee suggested another £1.4 million in cuts. Both Winterhill and the marble bus station sites were described as white elephants. The focus of transport hubs so far from the centre had been dictated by the city's planned location next to the West Coast railway line.

The *Milton Keynes on Sunday* report continued: 'Policy committee chairman Councillor Nigel Long said: "My understanding is that it is a very good deal for the council. The Liberals have offered no alternative budget this year or for the last seven years. All they want to do is sit and criticise but offer no solutions."'

Robert Cook met with MK Metro's General Manager, Duncan Allen, in April 2000. Duncan explained the difficulties of recruiting drivers in Milton Keynes because the cost of living, especially housing, had risen dramatically since government policy had sold off council housing.

There are serious challenges for bus operators in this area, with many names disappearing in an age of reduced subsidy. Massive schools have provided a new source of revenue, but the age of coach excursions has become much reduced. Students are a limited new market because many attending Buckinghamshire's two universities are car users.

The sale of state assets dismembered the National Bus Company, resulting in no promised competition and reduced services in many areas. The Wycombe Bus Company, like Aylesbury Bus, was one short-term manifestation of the privatisation intended to promote competition, better services and lower fares. It was set up in November 1990 and liquidated in 2004.

Arriva is now the dominant operator in Buckinghamshire, with operational control based in Leicester. The company that became Arriva was founded by a former Sunderland steel worker, T. S. Cowie. He started out repairing and selling old bicycles for men to go job hunting. He branched out into second-hand motorcycles in 1938 as a dealer, trading as T. Cowie Limited.

After wartime service in the RAF he tried for a motorcycle dealership, but was blocked by snobbery. Luckily, the Italians were looking for dealers to sell their new motor scooters. In 1948, the business was relaunched by the founder's son, Tom Cowie. T. Cowie Ltd was floated in December 1964. A car dealership and the first of many buses followed in 1965.

Having created Britain's largest contract hire business in 1972, Cowie's went heavily into buses, buying Grey Green from the London-based George Ewer Group in 1980. Large vehicle-leasing companies Marley, Roy Scot Ringway and the Hanger Group were added in 1984. After Tom Cowie retired the company was renamed Cowie Group plc in April 1994.

Bus deregulation offered Arriva further opportunities, with the acquisition of Leaside Buses and the South London Transport businesses in January 1994 and January 1995.

United Automobile Services and British Bus were bought in July and August 1996, both having acquired a number of privatised bus companies. In October 1996, Cowie Group was reclassified on the stock exchange from a motor dealer to a transport group.

The new name Arriva plc was applied in November 1997, and the company was rebranded. That year, Arriva also bought Denmark's Unibus, paving the way to multinational status. The group began selling off motor vehicle businesses, moving into rail franchises and taking on the LNWR rail maintenance works in April 2008. Given the railway interests of the parent company Deutsche Bahn, the railway bias was inevitable.

In 2010, it was reported that the government-owned railway companies of France (SNCF) and Germany (Deutsche Bahn) were considering making takeover bids for the business of SNCF subsidiary Keolis. In April 2010, Deutsche Bahn made a takeover offer for Arriva at £7.75 a share (£1.585 billion). The takeover was approved by the European Commission in August 2010, conditional on Deutsche Bahn disposing of some Arriva services in Germany. The takeover took effect on 27 August 2010 and Arriva was delisted from the London Stock Exchange on 31 August 2010, becoming a subsidiary of Deutsche Bahn the same year.

Arriva operates bus, coach, train, tram and water bus services in fourteen countries across Europe. As of September 2018, it employed 61,845 people and carried 2.4 billion passenger journeys annually. It operates as three divisions: UK Bus, UK Rail and Mainland Europe. Deutsche Bahn announced in 2019 they wished to sell Arriva, but the sale was placed on hold in November that year.

In late 2011, Arriva acquired Grand Central and sold its Arriva Scotland West bus operation. In May 2013, Arriva purchased Veolia Transport's Central European business with 3,400 vehicles. Arriva changed its logo in January 2018.

The old UCOC bus depot in Aylesbury's Buckingham Road. Deregulation allowed takeover by Luton & District from January 1986. Their former enquiry shop is now a charity shop. The Leyland National is former UCOC 659. A Leyland Leopard with Plaxton Paramount coachwork occupies the garage forecourt. Demolished in May 1999, it was shortly to sprout with desirable dwellings, enabling more people to commute to London – furthering the town's dormitory function.

Bletchley, Queensway West, 5 April 1969. This UCOC Bristol FLF seventy-seater – 723 in the fleet – was new in 1967 and one of eight in a subgroup. It was withdrawn in 1979, as OMO buses were the new order in an age of declining bus travel. UCOC's Bletchley garage would be demolished following deregulation.

A Bristol K5G, number 721 in the UCOC fleet, with fifty-five-seater ECW body standing outside Stony Stratford Garage. New in 1947, it was withdrawn in 1963. The route blind number was misleading. This service bus ran between Wolverton and Buckingham.

This is the early 1960s. Lodekka 547 in the fleet proceeds sedately down the semi-pedestrianised Stony Stratford section of the A5 Watling Street. It was semi-pedestrianised once the A5D was opened. This bus was an LD6B with a sixty-seat ECW body new in 1958. (Andrew Shouler)

Stony Stratford's new bus station was built in 1963, with offices. This general view was taken in 1963. The site closed during deregulation. The main building survives as a car sales store, with the rest being surplus to Milton Keynes's new operator requirements and therefore sold off for profitable houses and flats. (Andrew Shouler)

UCOC Leyland National at the new Milton Keynes city centre in 1980, with a service to Bedford. The bus carries the National Bus logo and worked out of Winterhill. (Andrew Shouler)

Milton Keynes bus station was an extravagant, expensive design, using lots of marble. However, though close to the railway station, it was too far from the centre.

The UCOC Hitchin service waits at the ill-fated Milton Keynes bus station in 1980. Leyland had taken over AEC and Bristol, leaving little choice for bus operators. The National was meant to set a new standard for British service buses. It was not a comfortable ride all the way to Hitchin on this noisy, bouncy bus. (Andrew Shouler)

Roadcar's ex-National Bus Company Bristol VR crosses above a quintessential Milton Keynes market scene in 1994. This was another short-lived company name on the side of the local buses. Milton Keynes is a challenging environment because it was built for many things, but definitely not the bus.

Bletchley bus station, early 1980s. Milton Keynes is not a city, but it is cool to apply the City Bus Logo to this United Counties Bristol VR. This bus station is a windswept and cold place to be in winter. (Stephen Miller)

John Harper of Milton Keynes Council, left, and Graham Mabbutt, Milton Keynes Cabinet Member for Transport, right, in 2005. Behind them is a map of the Milton Keynes grid system. As the city expanded so did their challenges and opportunities. Graham said, 'Discouraging the private motorist from the central area has to be a priority if we are to get the best out of buses.'

A very nicely repainted and overhauled Bristol VR, number 798, stands in the Winterhill workshop in May 1984. It is awaiting its City Bus logo. Nowadays the site is occupied by Homebase, having been sold off cheap to boost council finances. (Andrew Shouler)

Tuesday 23 August 1983 at 9.25 a.m., and an excursion is about to set sail into the Cotswolds from Milton Keynes bus station. (Andrew Shouler)

Duncan Allan, General Manager of Milton Keynes MK Metro, in his Winterhill office, July 2000.

MK Metro's 1967 Leyland PD3 on the Buckingham–Milton Keynes route in 2000. The vehicle also doubled as a driver trainer.

Red Kite was another ephemeral bus operator emerging from the dust of 1985 deregulation. This ex-UCOC VR is on a school run heading south toward Winslow High Street in May 1999.

*Above*: Red Rose service at Central Milton Keynes in 1999. The name was revived from a pre-Second World War operator running between Aylesbury and Wendover. The new company recruited a former Red Rover employee who promoted use of the last ever Red Rover livery.

*Below*: Aberdeen-based First Bus was another major player post-deregulation but has disappeared from the county's bus routes. This vehicle was spotted on temporary park and ride services in October 1999.

# 8

# Next Stop

Buckinghamshire County Council issued the following statement when Covid-19 restrictions were lifted:

Buckinghamshire Council is encouraging residents to get back on board their local buses! Whether you're simply travelling to the nearest town centre or exploring further afield across the county and surrounding areas, there are various bus routes available for residents.

When COVID-19 hit, many bus routes were suspended, or only available to key workers. Now that we are heading back to normality, your local bus is ready and waiting for residents to get back on board!

Whether you're a commuter, a family or riding solo, bus companies offer a variety of tickets, including group tickets and multi-journey fares for those traveling by bus on a regular basis.

There are many benefits to taking the bus over going out in the car. A full double decker bus can take as many as 75 cars off the road, helping to reduce congestion on the roads and improving the environment. If you choose to take the bus, you can save money on fuel and parking, too – which could go towards an extra treat while you're out!

If you're commuting, catching the bus can give you a bit of downtime before work, allowing you to read a book, scroll through social media or watch some catch up TV on your phone.

Whatever your reason, one thing's for certain – Bucks is better by bus.'

Cabinet Member for Transport, Steve Broadbent said: 'Buses are a great way to get around the county and we would like to encourage people to give it a try and make use of the services available to them. Additionally, as demand on these routes expands, there is a great possibility to further our networks and enhance services to benefit both residents and our community. You can get some beautiful views of Buckinghamshire from the bus too! Just one of the many great reasons for getting the bus, not to mention the environmental difference you'll make too.'

Public transport provides a vital service for many. It is not easy to judge whether deregulation, breaking up the National Bus Company's components and allied asset stripping was ultimately a force for good. There is no knowing now what might have been.

The 1980s saw massive industrial contraction, job losses and a shrinking demand for bus services outside of London. Today bus fares are high relative to actual real income, unless a person has lived long enough to be eligible for a bus pass or young enough for school passes. These groups are the mainstays of the county, and country's, public transport system.

Against this background there is a good system radiating in and out of the county town of Aylesbury. The focal point for these services – the local bus station – opened in 1968, but it is showing its age in spite of numerous facelifts. It makes the more modern High Wycombe terminus seem like the Ritz.

Aylesbury bus station was described by one London visitor en route north, trying to see how far he could get in a day, as the most depressing place in the UK. He obviously needs to travel a bit more. The question is, where could a replacement go today? There is no way modern buses could fit in Kingsbury Square because single-deck buses carry far more passengers than 1960s double-deckers. Single-deckers, as one Arriva driver told me, are now 'like driving a giant brick'. The square is also too far from the inner ring road.

An assessment of where Bucks buses are now and what the future might offer might be best coming from studying small operators like Z&S and Red Rose. Buckinghamshire Council, like Milton Keynes unitary authority, has offered a number of initiatives.

After deregulation many town bus depots, like Aylesbury's ex-UCOC in Buckingham Street, became expensive town centre flats, with buses relocated to out of town centre industrial estates. There has been a lot of money made by selling off National Bus Company assets to private investors.

Barbara Castle was an enigmatic politician in her Transport Ministry role. In 1968, she signed off on closing the strategically important Oxford–Cambridge railway line because she considered it to be the age of the motor car. One assumes she was sincere in this belief. Therefore, she nationalised the buses to give them a sporting chance of keeping cars in check.

The Transport Act of 1968 increased permitted lorry gross weights, ending the era of mixed freight in trains of small railway wagons.

Buckinghamshire's historic railway towns of Bletchley and Wolverton in 1968 were swallowed up by what became Milton Keynes. Castle closed the Oxford–Cambridge passenger link for the beginning of the same year, filling the gap with a poor United Counties and City of Oxford Motor Services replacement operation. It faded away during the 1970s.

What started out as Milton Keynes no longer being the city of the motor car became an impossible challenge for comprehensive bus traffic without massive subsidies. Omnibus operations were to be returned to the profit motive at the outset of a new, demanding and uncertain age. Bus operators, freshly privatised, came and went, unable to compete with a car's convenience.

Had buses remained in full public ownership there would have been no need for massive directors' fees, bonuses and shareholder dividends. But there is always that quite difficult balance to achieve between a healthy, taxable, private sector and funding for the more mundane essentials.

In March 2019, Deutsche Bahn ('German Railway' in German), or DB for short, describes itself as the second-largest transport company in the world, after Deutsche Post AG, and is the largest railway operator and infrastructure owner in Europe. DB announced that it would be selling Arriva through either a sale or possible public flotation and then invited companies interested in acquiring it to register expressions of interest by 3 May 2019. However, by mid-November the sale was placed on hold.

At the time of writing, Arriva are rising to the climate change challenge. Arriva may suspect that a new bus boom is around the corner, funded by further massive public investment.

Undoubtedly deregulation has had some positive outcomes. Aylesbury has three dynamic smaller operators, namely Red Rose, Z&S and Redline. Red Rose was established by the late Chris Day and TaJ Khan using an historic local operator's name coupled to the final Red Rover livery. The founders had links with the redoubtable Red Rover Omnibus Company. Red Rose was established in the early 1990s, beginning with success on route seven, then expanding rapidly. It now offers services across the local counties.

Chris Day's family connection with buses traces back to involvement with the original Red Rose, which operated between Halton, Wendover and Aylesbury. Taj Khan had been a part-time Red Rover driver, where he became passionate about the industry. The partners saw potential in a business based on regular service, low fares and passenger comfort.

The company is currently based just outside Aylesbury in Dinton, with excellent maintenance facilities. They have a fleet of new vehicles covering public and school services in Buckinghamshire, Oxfordshire, Hertfordshire and Milton Keynes. Given the county's complexity, Red Rose have done rather well, benefiting from rapid Aylesbury and Milton Keynes expansion – a particular challenge and area of opportunity.

Sir Bob Reid was the last chairman of British Rail. Robert Cook interviewed him in 2006, during Bob's tenure as head of the Milton Keynes Partnership. The partnership was charged with overseeing the expansion of Milton Keynes. A great deal of the original open spaces were going to be filled in, creating more roads and traffic. Robert Cook asked Sir Bob, 'Is public transport relevant to your goals?' He replied:

The work that has been done in the plan is a good intellectual piece of work and what it describes in the next twenty-five years is that people will be older and the community will be predominantly more single.

There will be more single people living in what were family houses for a variety of reasons, debt, separation, etc. These are the social trends that people see as being unavoidable and will influence how the city is going to look. Equally it is clear as people get older they will be less able or keen to drive themselves. This has two implications, one they'll want the services they need for their day to day life to be available to them, close to where their homestead is. They will want a medical service, a health service, all the things like beauty parlours, hairdressing salons, within the area they can walk. That has an implication on the design of the new development areas and has a major impact on how you position your regeneration. By design you are reducing dependence on the motor car and increasing reliance on public transport.

Another implication is that public transport becomes much more important. To get public transport going it has to be reliable, frequent, easy to use. And relatively affordable. London has done this with a much larger population, by giving the residents travel permits which are taken up in the money you pay for the rates. People get a document which they can use every day in the year, at certain times, and they can jump on a bus for nothing. They can jump on the Underground. On the surface you fill the place with buses taking people to where they want to go to.

One of the great faults of traffic designers is they take people where they don't want to go to. And the railways is no exception to this. Taking people to St Pancras when they want to be in Liverpool Street is not very sensible. So you've got to be sure the service does work and is effective.

A lot of work is going in on that now, to provide a bus service to build up public acceptance. To make sure people use it, they need to come off the train in MK, walk out and get on a bus that will take them up to the business centre; or at Bletchley and they want to go to a football match, they come off the train and jump on a bus. You make your services to meet your needs. That piece of work is not simple. It's not a question of the vehicle you use. If you are not a tram-type city like Amsterdam or Melbourne with a long street you just go up and down you have to develop buses.

Compared to other major towns and cities in Britain, it's easy to get around by car, but expansion is changing things.

Sir Bob Reid and his MK Partnership Committee faced the task of shifting locals and visitors away from motor cars. Not an easy task. The situation is still problematic, with ever more people and congestion.

Aylesbury bus station opened in 1968 in the bowels of the new Friars Square shopping centre, which housed Europe's largest branch of Woolworths over three floors. Drivers often have to park wherever they can.

Aylesbury High Street, September 2021. Red Rose have made excellent improvements to their fleet. Aylesbury bus station sees some very good coverage of a wide and challenging mix of urban and rural locations. This bus is heading out to Waddesdon and Steeple Claydon.

Aylesbury bus station, August 2021. Arriva are now the major county-wide service provider, taking over from UCOC, with Red Rose the new Red Rover and wearing the same red and yellow livery. This image of Aylesbury bus station also shows social distancing due to Covid-19 measures.

MK Metro Bletchley 14 service at Central Milton Keynes, December 2001. Passengers are disembarking for late-night shopping.

Stony Stratford Tram Terminus, *c.* 1920. How did we get from here to now? The direction sign on the lamppost offers the choice of London, Birmingham or Oxford. This view may be charming, but life was grim for most. The tramline was built as a cheap, reliable means of transporting workers to the LNWR, later LMS, railway coach building and maintenance works at Wolverton.

*Above*: This was the old UCOC maintenance shop at Milton Keynes, Winterhill. It was taken over by MK Metro, part of the Status Group and one of the beneficiaries of 1985 deregulation. Arriva bought MK Metro for £5.6 million in 2005. Here we see a fitter repairing their Northern Counties-bodied former GM Leyland Olympian double-decker, which had been in a collision with a car, seen here in April 2000. The Winterhill site was sold off cheaply to boost Milton Keynes' depleted finances.

*Below*: Stagecoach X49, Central Milton Keynes, 1998.

*Above*: Central Milton Keynes, the X4 to Peterborough, in 2004, with Stagecoach displaying their new livery.

*Below*: Virgin's express coach service from Central Milton Keynes to Luton Airport, 1999.

No one will miss these brightly painted Alexander Dennis double-deckers. Stagecoach's latest livery photographed on 23 October 2021 in Buckingham. The two buses are on the X5 – one to Oxford and the other returning to Bedford. The service formerly ran through to Cambridge.

Aylesbury offers two services to Oxford – the 280 Arriva's longest route. This image shows the more direct X20 provided by Redline waiting outside Aylesbury railway station. The journey takes around sixty minutes depending on traffic.

An idyllic image of an Arriva double-decker approaching a little bus stop at Adstock on the A413, 6 April 2021. The shelter has been there since the 1950s.

A very crowded X60 service between Aylesbury and Milton Keynes in December 2021. It has just picked up schoolchildren, taking them from Winslow back to Buckingham. Meanwhile, the same time service from Buckingham brings schoolchildren back to Winslow.

Great names such as City of Oxford Motor Services (COMS) are long gone from Aylesbury. The Oxford Bus Company came into being, but never reached Aylesbury. Arriva filled the breach, supported by Redline's X20 Express.

Arriva are a world beyond the old world. All buses and coaches have Wi-Fi and automatic vehicle location (AVL) equipment installed, which works via GPS technology. The AVL equipment installed on each bus or coach gives geographical location to within a few metres and is updating central control room every few seconds. This can therefore be seen in real time at the central control room, which helps in managing the fleet. Updates are then relayed to illuminated boards at select bus stops.

Cameras are now fitted in buses and there is also a driver radio contact to base, which are both there for health and safety. Rural routes lack late night services, so if travellers are out late the only options are walking or calling a taxi. Sunday services are significantly reduced too.

In Robert Cook's childhood and youth local buses ran as late as 11 p.m. Those were the days of two-man services and open platforms. The Winslow–Aylesbury fare was 7.5p in 1962. It now costs over £5 for a return ticket. There are no more bus conductors either, with all of their camaraderie and attention to passengers.

Many will recall the good old days on the late bus from Aylesbury in the 1960s. There was an exciting atmosphere on Aylesbury's Kingsbury Square, with its pubs and cafés, like Mrs Grundy's. All the bright lights, glittering shop windows, playful youths and the lazy beat of heavy diesel engines. Greenlines ran late into Aylesbury, parking in a Buckingham Street lay-by. The town thronged with life and an excellent fish and chip shop was always busy.

These ways faded slowly, and then suddenly they were gone. The future will not be a return to the past. Arriva, Stagecoach, Red Rose, Z&S and Redline are faring well, but could not thrive without school passengers subsidised by Buckinghamshire Council. Concessions to the elderly are another contribution of 19p per trip. These people make up the bulk of passengers.

But with London looking to tax cars out of the centre, other major towns might follow. Bucks' car drivers may not be prepared to go along with this. It has been noted that the problem in London is that too many motorists have been paying the congestion and non-compliant engine fees.

There is no doubt that motoring will face increasing restrictions and rules. Currently, most councils are only able to send out penalties for parking and driving in bus lanes. More restrictions, higher tax, parking issues and rising fuel bills may boost bus usage. Fewer cars mean more bus passengers. This could mean lower subsidies or lower fares. The Department for Transport (DfT) reports:

Outside London, the local bus industry is deregulated, but London runs an entirely tendered bus market under the oversight of Transport for London. Comparisons with London and the rest of country should be made with considerable care. In English non-metropolitan areas, Bus Service Operators Grant (BSOG) per passenger journey was 12.9 pence in the year ending 2015 and 8.5 pence in English metropolitan areas. Subsidies account for about 45 per cent of bus operators revenues.

BSOG is a grant paid to operators of eligible bus services and community transport organisations to help them recover some of their fuel costs. The amount each bus operator receives is based on their annual fuel consumption. BSOG also aims to benefit passengers by helping operators keep fares down and enabling operators to run services that might otherwise be unprofitable and could lead to cancellation.

In the year ending 2015 the average level of bus subsidy (direct from central government) per passenger journey was 5.4 p. This had decreased (adjusted for inflation) from 10.8 p in the year ending March 2005. The rate at which BSOG is paid was cut by 20 per cent from April 2012.

Payments are also made to local authorities for running bus services. These sums are broadly equivalent to BSOG payments previously paid to authorities for running section 19 community transport services in-house and bus operators for running services under tender to local authorities. The figures exclude expenditure on capital projects (e.g. bus lane priority schemes), which benefit the bus industry directly or indirectly.

Since the 2010 general election a combination of cuts to local authority budgets, changes to the administration of concessionary bus travel and reductions to BSOG has raised concerns that the local bus network in England could be severely cut back in the future.

The following is extracted from a DfT report:

While there is some evidence of this [cuts], the Government has pointed to improvements in other areas and increased financial support for green buses and bus partnerships. In line with its broader localism agenda Government has also announced intention to devolve some BSOG funding to local authorities and to further reform BSOG in 2014. Concessionary fares are something else and complex.

In 2019/20, 4.07 billion passenger journeys were made by local bus in England, down 238 million journeys or 5.5 per cent when compared with 2018/19. The fall can largely be attributed to the effects of passenger journeys from COVID-19 in the last quarter of 2019/20. While the national lockdown only began on 23rd March and covered a small proportion of the year, bus companies reported they started seeing declines in journeys in the preceding weeks.

The number of local bus passenger journeys in England fell by 238 million or 5.5% to 4.07 billion in the year ending March 2020. Bus mileage in England decreased by 3.1% when compared with 2018/19.

The fall increased by 2.5 billion or 61% to 1.57 billion in the year ending March 2021. The fall can largely be attributed to nationwide movement restrictions introduced throughout 2020/21 in response to the coronavirus pandemic. The Covid-19 bus service support grant (CBSSG) was introduced to keep bus services running that may otherwise have operated at a loss or not at all.

Lower subsidy per passenger journey will indicate better value for the public purse. However, this could arise as a result of reductions to the most heavily subsidised services – many of which would be unprofitable without public subsidy – risking making rural communities more isolated.

The official attitude to Covid-19 impact and service decline is revealing of the government's priorities, based on expediency rather than need for sustainable, sound, enduring public transport.

The national system struggled in the years running up to deregulation. Milton Keynes became a magnet for long-distance travel. Alder Valley and United Counties ran a joint service between Milton Keynes and Reading. It ran via Maidenhead, starting in October 1983. The following November, an Aylesbury–London service was started. It was mainly aimed at RAF Halton personnel. Red Rover tried to get in on United Counties' services to Wendover on the spurious basis of contact with Wendover market. Bucks County Council intervened to block this.

There has clearly been conflict between the need for regulations and the need for freedom, which transport should facilitate. Then there is the money issue. Amersham & District's former manager Bill Kirby told Robert Cook in 1994: 'We flew by the seat of our pants in the 1930s. I was a young man in the office, with engine blocks and parts laying all about the place.' In the early years it was up to the buccaneers.

Buccaneers like the men who created Buckinghamshire's Red Rover and Wellingborough's United Counties broke the rules in early years. The rule makers soon caught up. Along came deregulation and state-built assets were sold off. Money was made for the city slickers and a few opportunists.

There have, however, been considerable efforts and improvements to national and local transport. Bucks County Council promoted the Sunday Rover ticket. For little more than £5 a person could travel all over the South East and East Anglia. But it was poorly publicised and so faded away.

When Milton Keynes came into being, planners struggled to come up with a workable solution to so much of the old United Counties (UCOC)meandering rural stomping ground being concreted over by new Milton Keynes development. As yet to be privatised, UCOC struggled with the idea of a 250-vehicle operation around Milton Keynes, having only the Stony Stratford and Bletchley depots. And so, Winterhill was built and handed over to United Counties on 1 March 1983. It was built by the Sir Robert MacAlpine company.

Competition and economy were promised on the buses post-1985, but there has been much money wasted and an increase in bureaucracy. Raising the status of buses is important to serious improvements.

There is a market, but there will always be need for some regulation and subsidy, as with railways. Investors want returns. Arriva is multinational, which complicates matters. Aylesbury depot operates fifty vehicles, the longest route being the winding village route via Thame to Oxford. Route planning for Buckinghamshire is made from the company's Leicester depot. Long rural routes like the X60 (run by Milton Keynes and Aylesbury depots) from Aylesbury to Milton Keynes, via Buckingham, are potential loss makers. Fare prices have to be carefully calculated, with large discounts on returns impossible, but County Rover tickets offer good value, covering multiple daily journeys. Express coaches are the new stagecoaches in a crucial new stage of public transport.

The county area was reduced by local government reforms in 1974, but the swell of population moving north, including massive Milton Keynes expansion, has created new and ongoing challenges. Though the county has its vast country estates with stately

Bletchley bus station on a bright spring day, March 2022. No doubt Ed Grimsdale would approve of this open-air facility in a suburb where space was abundant during Milton Keynes planning stages. From here it is possible to take bus and coach trips to all major county centres, most rural locations and the nation beyond. The old United Counties bus garage once stood next door, then came a pub, and now a new block of flats is underway. Reconstruction work for the soon to be restored east–west rail link is visible in the background, along with the cement works where block trains are loaded. The bus station has open-air windswept passenger shelters and is freezing in winter. Fortunately, local bus services are frequent.

homes like Chequers, far more people are living on limited and expensive reducing land area per head of population. Many struggle for a living. The current fuel crisis may have positive and negative impacts on bus use, possibly with the added danger of more Covid restrictions at time of writing.

In spite of massive residential development dating from the late nineteenth century, there is still much simple beauty and much history to be seen by riding buses around South Bucks.

Bus design and technology has made considerable advances toward meeting passenger needs. Between 1953 and 1973, London Transport's Amersham Garage, formerly Amersham & District, operated ten little Guy Specials on back road routes, running out to Beaconsfield, Buckland Common, Winchmore Hill and a vital service between Rickmansworth and Harefield Hospital. Painted green, they were a perfectly fit for the hilly landscape's windy lanes, villages and awkward old roads.

Riding service 300 from Aylesbury to High Wycombe takes us to Hughenden Valley, sighting Disraeli's old manor home and passing RAF Strategic Command front gates where a preserved Spitfire fighter stands on a plinth, as if in flight, symbolising Britain's freedom.

Travelling North from Aylesbury on the meandering 150 service we see another glimpse of tiny Buckinghamshire, dominated by Milton Keynes. The north has the River Ouse, sluggish and dull, and the M1 motorway ideal for express coaches.

The south, at High Wycombe, is only a few miles from the M40, bursting with development and convenient for London. Somewhere in between is demure polite Maidenhead, Cookham and the shimmering wealthy world of the River Thames. There is so much diversity in such a small piece of England. Arriva has its master plan directed from its Leicester headquarters. Smaller companies are there to fill in the gaps. It is a tough industry. Recent Arriva strikes denote the tension. Deregulation was intended to make all things better, along with rail privatisation – the absolute opposite of Labour's 1945 nationalising idealism. These are uncertain times. Who knows where the next stop will be?

# Acknowledgements

The authors would like to thank the following: Duncan Allen, *Buckingham Advertiser*, Bucks Council, *Bucks Herald*, *The Citizen*, Department For Transport, Edward Grimsdale, Mick Hayward, William Kirby, Dennis Mauger, Milton Keynes Unitary Authority, Milton Keynes Partnership, *Milton Keynes on Sunday*, Graham Mabutt, Stuart Mills, John Payne, Red Rose Omnibus Company, Sir Bob Reid, Andrew Shouler, R. H. G. Simpson and John Skinner.

All images are the authors' work and collections unless otherwise stated.

We extend thanks to all who have supplied photographs over the years. Special thanks to Andrew Shouler and R. H. G. Simpson.

# Bibliography

Martin, Andrew, *North Buckinghamshire*
Cook, Robert, *More of Milton Keynes: Building On The Vision*
Cook, Robert, *The Red Rover Story*
Cook, Robert and Andrew Shouler, *The United Counties Story*
Shorter, Clement and F.L. Griggs, *Highways & Byways of Buckinghamshire*

An Aylesbury-bound X30 Express service waiting departure at High Wycombe bus station, November 2022.